Charles J. Howe

The Deaf Mutes of Canada

A History fo their Education, with an Account of the Deaf Mute Institutions

Charles J. Howe

The Deaf Mutes of Canada
A History fo their Education, with an Account of the Deaf Mute Institutions

ISBN/EAN: 9783337187262

Printed in Europe, USA, Canada, Australia, Japan

Cover: Foto ©ninafisch / pixelio.de

More available books at **www.hansebooks.com**

THE
DEAF MUTES OF CANADA.

A HISTORY OF THEIR EDUCATION,

WITH AN ACCOUNT OF THE

DEAF MUTE INSTITUTIONS OF THE DOMINION,

AND A DESCRIPTION OF ALL KNOWN

FINGER AND SIGN ALPHABETS.

NUMEROUS   *ILLUSTRATIONS.*

TORONTO:
C. J. HOWE, PUBLISHER.
1888.

PREFACE.

THE volume here presented to the reader contains a full *resume* of the most interesting facts concerning the Deaf-mute World. Compiled in part from many sources, it will be found to offer in an interesting form all that readers in general will care to know To Canadians in particular the detailed account of the commencement of deaf-mute education in this country, written by one closely connected with the work from the beginning, will be found of special interest, and will place on permanent record many facts that would otherwise have been lost. It will be valued by all connected with the work in the past, and to the first generation of educated Canadian deaf-mutes, now scattered throughout the Dominion, the narrative and illustrative reminders of their earlier years, will, we are sure, be eagerly welcomed.

To those hitherto unacquainted with the position and needs of deaf-mutes we hope the book will be of service in arousing an active interest in their behalf. No class needing so much, in many circumstances, the aid of intelligent sympathizers. In the words of Mr. Mathison, Superintendent of the Institution at Belleville " Uneducated, a deaf child has no knowledge of language ; is isolated, as it were, from the rest of mankind ; is irresponsible and in many cases dangerous to the community; life is a blank without a ray of hope to illuminate the future. With an education such as may be had here, all this is changed and the mute is enabled to take his or her place as respectable members of society and law-abiding citizens and learn of the glorious life beyond." Who that has the power would not willingly contribute towards such results, and it cannot be too widely known " that the Institution for the Deaf and

DEAF MUTE EDUCATION.

Dumb at Belleville is open to the deaf children of the Province, and every deaf-mute child in Ontario, whether the parents are poor or rich, may share in the many advantages the Institution affords, such as tuition, board, care, etc. There are many friends of such children who do not know of this place, and persons who will inform them of what the Province has so generously provided for their children will confer a lasting obligation.

CHAS. J. HOWE.

TORONTO, March, 1888.

CONTENTS.

PART I.

GENERAL HISTORY OF DEAF-MUTE EDUCATION.

	PAGE.
CHAPTER I.	
Origin and Progress of Deaf-Mute Education ...	9
CHAPTER II.	
Deaf-Mute Alphabets...	16
CHAPTER III.	
The Uneducated Deaf-Mute—The Sign Language—The Difficulties in the Acquisition of Language—The Deaf-Mute's and the Armenian's Letters—From the Creature to the Creator ...	26
CHAPTER IV.	
Anecdotes of Deaf-Mutes—A Deaf-Mute's Prayer—The Finger and Sign Language Utilized—Jesus and Me—Deaf-Mute Artists—A Prodigy—Deaf-Mute Compositions—Massieu and Clerc—Absurd Expectations...	35
CHAPTER V.	
The Systems of Instruction ...	41
CHAPTER VI.	
The Mental and Moral Condition of the Uneducated Deaf-Mutes—No Ideas of a Creator—Is Conscience Primitive?...	42
CHAPTER VII.	
Marriages Among Deaf-Mutes ...	47
CHAPTER VIII.	
Blind Deaf-Mutes—Laura Bridgman—Mary Bradley—Joseph Hague—Anecdotes—Death of Hague—Other cases on Record ...	57
CHAPTER IX.	
An Easy Method of Teaching Deaf-Mutes at Home...	71

PART II.

HISTORY OF DEAF-MUTE EDUCATION IN CANADA.

CHAPTER I.	
History of Deaf-Mute Education in Ontario ...	78
CHAPTER II.	
History of the Deaf-Mute Education in Quebec ...	105
CHAPTER III.	
History of Deaf-Mute Education in Nova Scotia ...	125

LIST OF ILLUSTRATIONS.

Title page of Bonet's Book	Frontispiece
Abbe Sicard	10
Statue of De L'Epee	12
Laurent Clerc	13
Old Hartford Institution	14
New Hartford Institution	14
National Deaf-Mute College	15
St. Ann's Church, New York	15
Bonet's Alphabet	17
One Hand Alphabet	19
Two Hand Alphabet	20
Dalgarno's Alphabet	21
Alphabeto Manuale	23
Military and Naval Sign Alphabet	24
Laura Bridgman	50
Letter by Laura Bridgman	55
Mary Bradley	61
Bradley and Hague Blind Deaf-mutes	65
Mr. J. B. McGann	78
Phoebe Street School	81
Old Grammar School, Jarvis Street	83
Queen St. School	84
Brock St. Boarding House	88
Little Richmond Street School	89
Florence Block, Hamilton	93
Dundurn Castle	96
Mr. J. J. G. Terrill	99
Earlham Cottage	99
Belleville Institution	100
Main Street School, Hamilton	102
Mr. J. B. McGann's Monument	103
Mr. Thomas Widd	116
First Protestant Deaf-Mute School in Montreal	119
Mackay Institution, Montreal	104
Halifax Institution	120

8

DEAF-MUTE EDUCATION.

CHAPTER I.

ORIGIN AND PROGRESS OF DEAF-MUTE EDUCATION.

THE following excellent sketch of the history of the earliest labors in behalf of the deaf is mainly taken from one of the Reports to the Government of Ontario, written by Mr. Mathison, Supt. of the Ontario Institution, and in commencing a general account of Deaf-mute Education, a more accurate and concise narration could not be presented to the reader:

"The education of the deaf has claimed the attention of great minds for many years, and the efforts of those engaged in the work at present are earnest and effective. In the early ages deaf-mutes were considered incapable of instruction, and were debarred from the rights of citizenship.

"Aristotle laid it down in his writings 'that of all the senses hearing contributes the most to intelligence and knowledge, and that the deaf are wholly incapable of intellectual instruction.' Notwithstanding this, instances are recorded where deaf and dumb persons have become eminent in various walks of life, and we have some in Ontario to-day who rank among our most intellectual citizens. In the fifteenth century, Jerome Cardan, an eminent man of that time, after paying considerable attention to the subject, came to the conclusion that 'the instruction of the deaf and dumb is difficult but it is possible.' History gives the credit of systematic teaching of the deaf and dumb to Pierre de Ponce, a Benedictine Monk of Spain, and to that country belongs the honor of having the three first teachers of this class. Thomas Braidwood, a Scotchman, in 1760, taught a few pupils whose friends were in a position to pay large fees, and thus established the first regular school for deaf-mutes in Great Britain. The first institution for the deaf, free to all, and supported by Government, was opened at Leipsic in 1778. The early instructors of the deaf and dumb in Great Britain were unwilling to reveal their modes of teaching unless their very exorbitant terms were complied with, consequently it was only children of comparatively wealthy people who could obtain an education. When the late Dr. Gallaudet visited England in 1815 for the purpose of gaining information with the view of establishing a school at Hartford, he found it impossible to induce the possessor of the art to part with their secrets. At this time, however, the instruction of the deaf and dumb

DEAF MUTE EDUCATION.

THE ABBE SICARD.

had made great strides in France, and he was welcomed there by the celebrated Sicard who gave him every assistance in qualifying himself for the contemplated work in America.

"Sicard at the time of Dr. Gallaudet's visit was head of the Institution Nationale of Paris. He had received his training under the famous De l' Epee, *le pere des sourdes-mutes*. This benevolent man, whose name must always occupy a prominent place in any account of the progress of Deaf-mute Education, commenced his life work in the year 1760, with little foreknowledge of the work he was entering upon. The manner in which his attention was first drawn to the deaf is related in the following interesting passage from an address of Mr. Clerc :—

"'A lady, whose name I do not recollect, lived in Paris, and had among her children two daughters, both deaf and dumb. The Father Vanin, one of the members of the Society of Christian Doctrine, was acquainted with the family, and attempted, without method, to supply in these unfortunate persons the want of hearing and speech; but was surprised by a premature death before he could attain any degree of success. The two sisters as well as the mother were inconsolable at

DEAF MUTE EDUCATION.

that loss, when, by Divine Providence, a happy event restored everything. The Abbe de l'Epee, formerly belonging to the above-mentioned society, had an opportunity of calling at their house. The mother was abroad, and while he was waiting for her he wished to enter into conversation with the young ladies; but their eyes remained fixed on their needles, and they gave no answer. In vain did he renew his questions; in vain did he redouble the sound of his voice; they were still silent, and durst hardly raise their heads to look at him. He did not know that those whom he thus addressed were doomed by nature never to hear or speak. He already began to think them impolite and uncivil, and rose to go out. Under these circumstances the mother returned, and everything was explained. The good Abbe sympathized with her on her affliction, and withdrew, full of the thought of taking the place of Father Vanin.

"'The first conception of a great man is usually a fruitful germ. Well acquainted with the French grammar, he knew that every language was a collection of signs, as a series of drawings is a collection of figures, the representation of a multitude of objects, and that the deaf and dumb can describe everything by gestures, as you paint everything with colors, or express everything by words; he knew that every object had a form, that every form was capable of being imitated; that action struck your sight, and that you are able to describe them by imitative gestures; he knew that words were conventional signs, and that gestures might be the same, and that there could therefore be a language formed of gestures, as there was a language of words.

"'Full of these fundamental ideas, the Abbe de l'Epee was not long without visiting the unfortunate family again, and with what pleasure was he not received! He reflected, he imitated, he delinated, he wrote; believing he had but a language to teach, while in fact he had two minds to cultivate! How painful, how difficult were the first essays of the inventor! Deprived of all assistance, in a career full of thorns and obstacles, he was a little embarrassed, but was not discouraged. He armed himself with patience and succeeded, in time, to restore his pupils to society and religion.'

"De l'Epee's success with these two pupils led him to seek for others, and he soon gathered round him a number of mutes in a humble establishment at Montmartre, to whose welfare he devoted the rest of his life. One instance out of many on record will testify to the whole hearted devotion of this good man to the main object of his existence. In his old age and during a severe winter, denied himself the comfort

DEAF MUTE EDUCATION.

MARTIN'S STATUE OF DE L'EPEE AT THE PARIS INSTITUTION.

of a fire in his own apartment; the remonstrances of his friends and the entreaties of his pupils were long unavailing. When at last he yielded to the tears of the children, he often reproached himself with selfishness; looking around mournfully he would say: 'My poor children, I have wronged you of a hundred crowns.'

DEAF MUTE EDUCATION.

"A statue to the memory of De l'Epee was erected in the garden of the Paris Institution, May 24th, 1879. It was executed and presented by a deaf-mute sculptor of the name of Martin. It represents the Abbe teaching a deaf-mute the Divine name which is inscribed with its dactylologic representation on a tablet which he holds in his hand.

LAURENT CLERC.

"As the result of the mission of Dr. Gallaudet, Mr. Clerc, one of Sicard's favorite pupils, and a man of eminent ability, was induced to return with him to America. Sicard parted with Clerc with reluctance, his assistance in the Paris Institution was highly valued, but with wide-minded benevolence Sicard permitted his departure in the spirit of the words written to introduce Clerc to Bishop Chevenis, of Boston, ' I would fain regard him as the apostle to the deaf-mutes of the New World.'

"Soon after the return of Dr. Gallaudet the Institution at Hartford was established, and from this has sprung many others, every State in the neighbouring Republic having its own school for the deaf. Among these the most prominent is the National Deaf-Mute College, at Washington. This College was established in 1864 as the highest department of the Columbia Institution, under the care of the National Government,

OLD HARTFORD INSTITUTION.

NEW HARTFORD INSTITUTION.

NATIONAL DEAF-MUTE COLLEGE.

and is presided over by Dr. Edward M. Gallaudet, youngest son of Dr. T. H. Gallaudet. The eldest son, the Rev. Dr. Thomas Gallaudet, is well known as the originator in 1850, and by general consent the head, of Church Work among the Deaf in America; his headquarters are at St. Ann's Church, West Eighteenth Street near Fifth Avenue, New York. It is interesting to note that a son of Mr. Clerc, the Rev. Dr. Francis J. Clerc, has also been engaged in this work; he was for several years pastor of the Mission in Philadelphia."

ST. ANN'S CHURCH, NEW YORK.

CHAPTER II.

DEAF-MUTE ALPHABETS.

The earliest sign alphabet of which we have any record is contained in a book by the Venerable Bede, printed in 1532, soon after the invention of printing. The title of the work is *De Loquela per Gestum Digitorium* ("On Speech by means of the Motion of the Fingers.") This is doubtless the first manual alphabet ever engraved. We do not know if any copy of this book is now obtainable, or its reproduction would be a matter of great interest. The next work in point of date bearing on this subject is a curious and valuable volume published in Madrid in 1620. It is the production of a Spanish monk named Juan Pablo Bonet. The work is entitled *Reduccion de las Letras y Arte para Ensenar a Hablar a los Mudos*. The illustrations are elaborate and of considerable size. The engravings of Bonet's alphabet, which we here print, faithfully represents on a reduced scale the shapes of the letters as given by him, dispensing with the highly ornamented border in which they are enclosed. The elaborate title-page of this book we have reproduced as a frontpiece to the present publication. Its symbolism will repay attention. The bird set free, and the unloosing of the tongue, representing the opening of the imprisoned mind and the gift of language to the dumb. Bonet's book fell into the hands of De l'Epee soon after he commenced his labors of love in educating the deaf, and with slight variations was adopted by him in his method of instruction. His eminent assistant and successor Sicard carried on and confirmed the use of this alphabet in France. Dr. Gallaudet and Sicard's pupil, Mr. Clerc, brought it with them to America where its use became universal among the various institutions that rapidly arose. Soon after he arrived in Hartford, Mr. Clerc sat to an artist for the purpose of having the letters accurately drawn, and he took advantage of the opportunity to make some slight improvements in the arrangement of the fingers. This alphabet, as now used, is given here. From its long continuance and all but universal use it is little likely to suffer any change in the future, and to Bonet justly belongs the credit of giving to the deaf-mute world an alphabet so nearly perfect in its first construction as to be little capable of subsequent improvement.

The knowledge of Bonet's work in Spain was early communicated to some learned men at the University of Oxford by Sir Kenelm Digby,

DEAF MUTE EDUCATION.

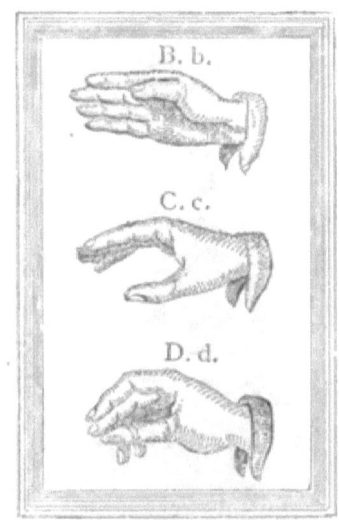
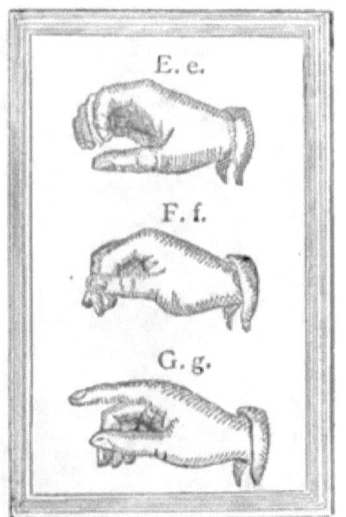
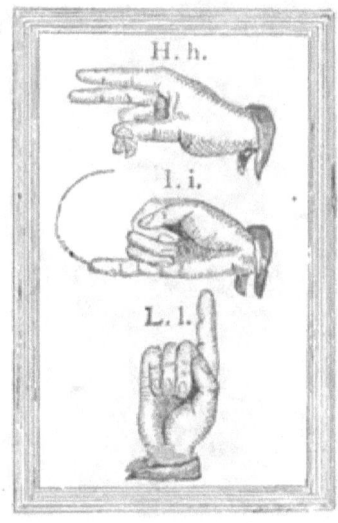

BONET'S ALPHABET.

DEAF MUTE EDUCATION.

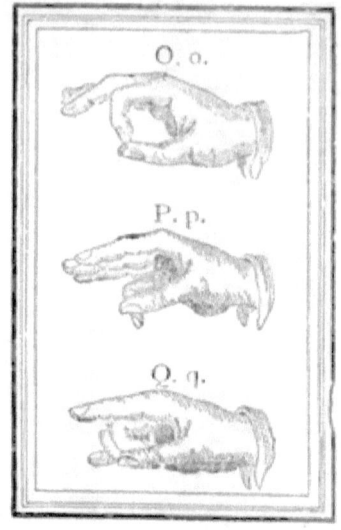
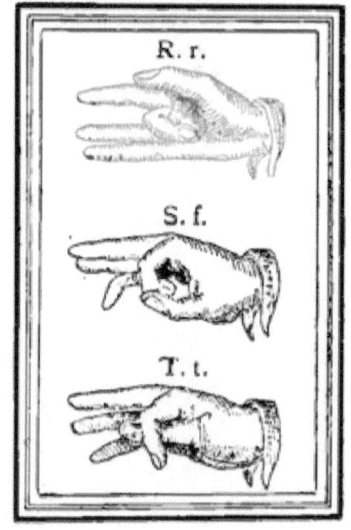

BONET'S ALPHABET.

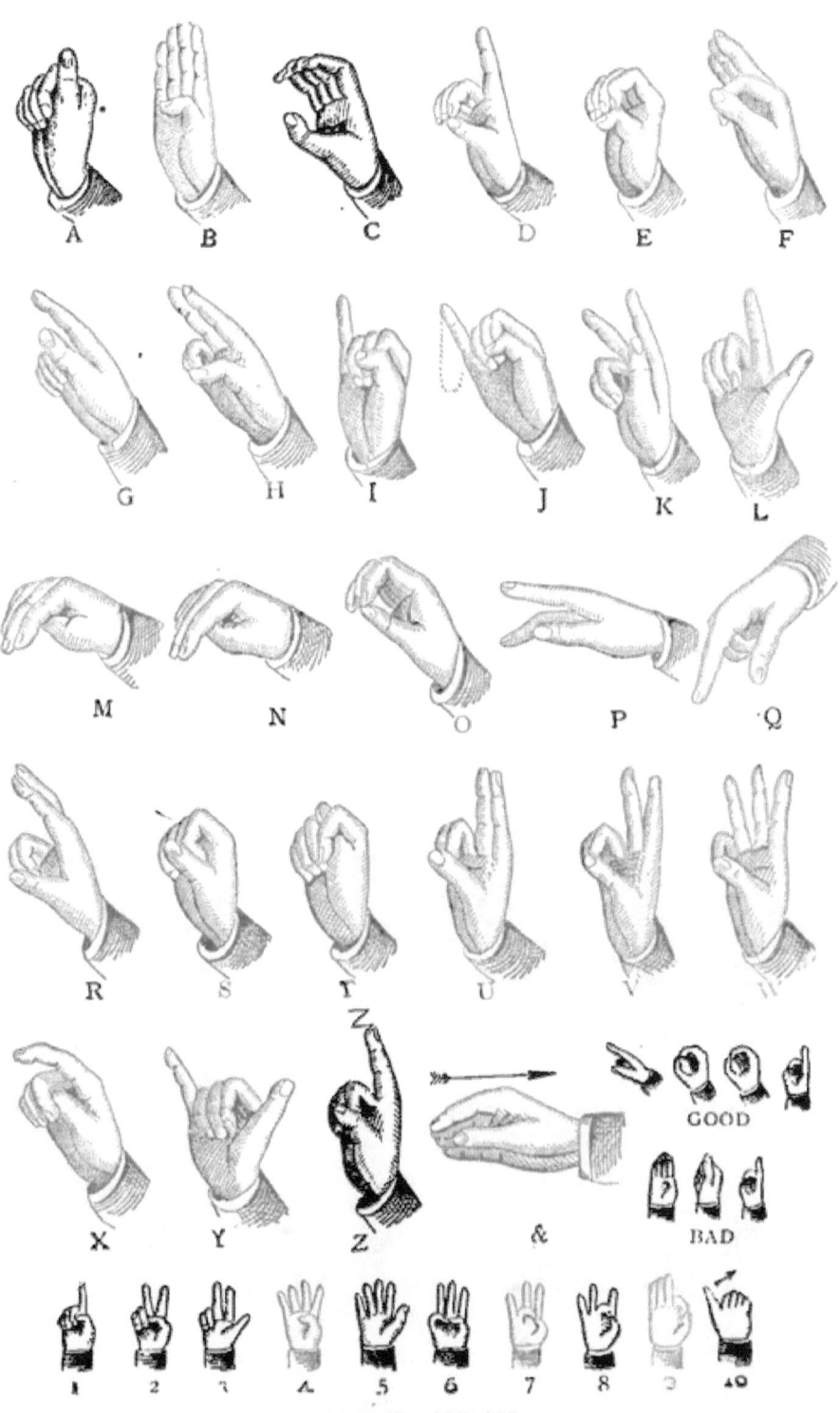

ONE-HAND ALPHABET.

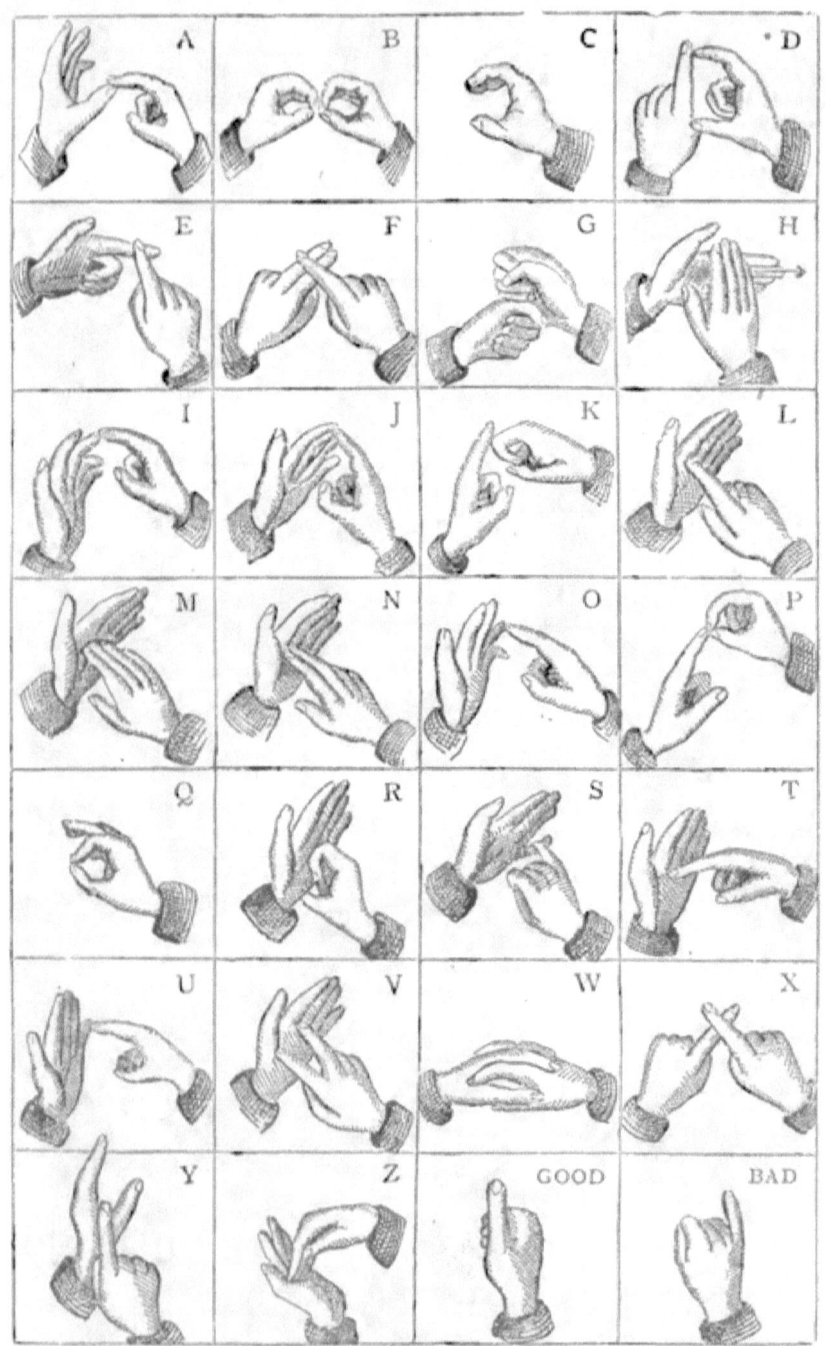

TWO-HAND ALPHABET.

a companion of Charles I., when Prince of **Wales, on** his romantic journey to Madrid in 1623. Some of Bonet's pupils **were** shown to the Prince and his companions, and Sir Digley relates **some** wonderful tales of their power of conversing with one another at a distance. Amongst those whose attention **was** attracted to the subject by Sir Digby **was**

an Aberdeen Scotchman, at that time **master of a Grammar School at** Oxford, by name **George** Dalgarno. **He wrote and** published a **book in** 1680, called "*Didascalocophus*, or the Deaf and Dumb Man's Tutor." In this book he gives an account of an alphabet **of his** own devising in which **the** letters are arranged on the fingers and palm of **the** hand. The accompanying illustration will give an accurate idea of this system. As will be observed it is likely to be far from clear in practice, and the indication of the vowels by touching the tops of the fingers **is** the only part of Dalgarno's alphabet that has been retained in use.

In the Deaf-mute Institutions of Great Britain a two handed alphabet is used, of the origin of which **we have no** trace. Perhaps the work of the **Venerable** Bede previously referred to might afford **some light on** this point. This alphabet has the advantage of great clearness. **The** positions of the hands indicate the **shapes** of Capital letters except in the case of vowels which are represented as in Delgarno's **method.** Signs have been invented to represent **the** shapes of the vowels as well as the consonants, but the most common practice of touching **the** tops **of the fingers is** preferable as enabling the deaf more readily to remember which letters are vowels.

A is expressed by touching the top of the thumb of the left hand, with the forefinger of the right.

B. Join **the** forefinger **and thumb of** each hand, and place the backs of the forefinger nails together.

C. Bend the fingers and **thumb of the left** hand, so **as to** form three parts of a circle.

D. Bend the fingers and thumb of the right hand into a semicircle and then join them to the forefinger of the left, which keep in a straight line.

E. Touch the top of the forefinger of the left hand with the forefinger of the right.

F. Place the forefinger of the right hand across the backs of the first and second fingers of the left.

G. Clench both hands, and put one fist upon the other.

H. Pass the palm of the right hand across that of the left, sweeping it along to the tips of the fingers, as if brushing something off.

I. Touch the top of the second finger of the left hand with the forefinger of the right.

J. Make a "I" and then draw the forefinger of the right hand down to the palm of the left.

K. Form a semicircle with the thumb and forefinger of the right hand and join it to the forefinger of the left, which must be kept straight out, both forefingers must meet at the second joints.

L. Place the forefinger of the right hand across the centre of the palm of the left, so that the top of the finger may be exactly in the middle of the palm.

M. Place three fingers of the right hand flat upon the palm of the left.

N. Place two fingers of the right hand flat upon the palm of the left.

O. Touch the top of the third finger of the left hand with the forefinger of the right.

P. Place the tops of the forefinger and thumb of the left hand in a semicircular form against the first and second joints of the forefinger of the right, which should be kept straight.

Q. Form a circular with the forefinger and thumb of the left hand and then curve the forefinger of the right into the shape of a hoop, and place it exactly where the other fingers join.

R. Bend the forefinger of the right hand and rest it on the palm of the left.

S. Bend the little finger of each hand and lock them together.

T. Fix the tip of the forefinger of the right hand against the middle of the lower edge of the left.

U. Touch the top of the little finger of the left hand with the forefinger of the right.

V. Place the first and second fingers of the right hand apart, upon the palm of the left.

DEAF MUTE EDUCATION.

W. Lock the fingers of one hand between those of the other.

X. Cross the forefingers at the second joints.

Y. Extend the thumb and forefinger of the left hand, and at the lower part of the fork so made, place the forefinger of the right hand.

Z. Place the tips of the fingers of the right hand on the palm of the left.

The illustration of the "Alphabeto Manuale," which we here bring before the reader, represents a particularly ungraceful and incongruous alphabet in use in some parts of Italy and in Mexico. The object of this system would appear to be to prevent conversation by pupils without the observation of the teacher. Though some of the letters are represented by motions and positions of the fingers others are indicated by touching different parts of the face, pulling the ear, etc. It is far from pleasing in practice, and its relegation to a place amongst obsolete forms is much to be desired.

We conclude our notice of the various sign alphabets by reproducing from a rare print kindly loaned by Mr. Greene, of the Belleville Institction a system at one time in use for communication at a distance for military and naval purposes. The Telegraph, Electric Light and other improved methods have long superseded this antique alphabet, and though it might be still of some service in rare situations, we believe it has taken its place amongst the curiosities of the past.

NAVAL AND MILITARY SIGN ALPHABET.

CHAPTER III.

THE UNEDUCATED DEAF-MUTE—THE SIGN LANGUAGE—THE DIFFICULTIES IN THE ACQUISITION OF LANGUAGE—THE DEAF-MUTE'S AND THE ARMENIAN'S LETTERS—FROM THE CREATURE TO THE CREATOR.

With these alphabets the instruction of deaf-mutes became more general. Schools for them were established in most civilized countries. They became the key to the minds of these afflicted ones, and a kind of substitute for the potent "Ephphatha!" But to educate the deaf-mute appalling difficulties have to be surmounted. He knows no language, except a few gestures and simple signs. It is difficult for those not deaf to conceive of ideas without language. The most uncivilized savage has a language, and can express his ideas to those speaking his language. So the deaf-mute, until he acquires a knowledge of language, expresses his ideas in natural signs and gestures—the same as infants use. When a deaf-mute goes to a school for deaf and dumb children, his teacher has to supply both thought and language, and then to lay out and cultivate the many avenues to the mind over which thought goes and comes. His lessons involve much translation—first emotions into ideas, ideas into signs, and signs into written words, or words spelled out by the fingers letter for letter. Constant repetition is necessary to fix the words in the mind. The great difficulty is to get him to understand and remember words enough to convey his ideas as he writes or converses with hearing and speaking people. We now realize how much a child blessed with the gift of hearing and speech knows of language when he first goes to school—he has been taught by all the people he ever met by simply hearing them speak. But the only preparation the deaf-mute has received when he goes to school is his careful observation of the motions and behavior of people and things about him.

The difficulties besetting the progress of the deaf-mute are chiefly in the way of language. His means of expressing his wants and emotions are those which Darwin has shown to be common with the brute creation. His pantomines are no more like words than is the chatter of birds or the grimaces of a monkey. When his motions have been directed into the defined expression of thought his signs indicate ideas rather than the arbitrary symbols of speech. He has none of the benefits of comparative philology. All spoken language have certain semblances by which, knowing one language, the acquisition of others is facilitated. Yet, M. Hamerton, in his "Intellectual Life," says:

DEAF MUTE EDUCATION.

"A language cannot be throughly learned by an adult without five years residence in the country where it is spoken, and without close observation, a residence of twenty years is insufficent." This is not encouraging, but it is the truth. What then shall be expected of a deaf-mute, whose only opportunities for the acquirement of the English language are limited to the formulas of the class-room and occasional conversations with intelligent friends by pen or pencil? The first six or seven years in a deaf-mute's school life should be devoted to the study of language, —to obtain the key that unlocks to him the stores of human learning as contained in books. In this pursuit it is not the hundred thousand words of the dictionary that confuse the pupils, and dishearten the teacher, but the different uses to which the same words are put, and the different ideas depending simply on conjunction. Take as a simple illustration, the word "draw." The pupil is taught that a horse draws a waggon. The pantomine is clear and corresponds with his daily observation. But to his surprise, the next morning's paper, in its notices, says: "The concert drew a large house last night," and he has to learn that in this use draw means to attract, and house means a number of people. After being taught by pantomine to draw a picture, he is told if he is ever so fortunate as to have money on deposit, he must draw a check before he can get it. He has seen a school-mate draw a picture, but when the heroine of a modern novel "draws a sigh," his admiration for the capacity of art is increased. A magazine criticism commends the scenes of innocence and content which Milton "draw." but on reference to the parlor edition of "Paradise Lost," he finds no illustration, or only those which Gustave Dore has made. One must confess that the pupil has enough already to confuse him, but when, in addition, he is told that "a ship draws water," "a cook draws a fowl," a waiter draws a cork," money draws interest," and "a minister draws comparisons and references," he concludes in despair that the conundrums of language are things which no deaf-mute can find out. When to these numerous significations the modifying adverbs in, out, off, on, up, back, etc., are added, and when it is remembered that every peculiar use of a word must be made a special subject of instruction and retained by a special effort of memory, a keyhole perception may be obtained of the work involved in the education of a deaf-mute.

To illustrate the natural language of signs of the deaf and dumb in order that the reader may better understand it, let us suppose, for instance, that an uneducated deaf-mute had witnessed a drunken man

run over by a carriage and carried to the hospital or to his house; he would run home in a state of excitement, arrest his mother's attention, make the sign he had been using for man (probably by referring to his beard and showing his height), and then imitate his staggering gait as he went along: afterwards describing the galloping of a horse and the revolving of wheels as approaching the man, showing the shape of the vehicle as well as he could. He would then represent the man as being knocked down by it, showing over what part of the man's body they passed over by touching the part of his own. He would then make the sign for more men by holding up his fingers to denote the number; point to the door or shutter to describe the stretcher on which the injured man was carried, and imitate the carrying of something heavy on his shoulder, and the moving away of the crowd, by waving his hand in one direction. But he would not be able to tell the name of the street or place where this occurred, nor the name of the man injured, or that of the owner of the carriage;—nor would he be able to state anything that the people might have said about the affair, or any other details which a little hearing and speaking child would have been able to do. With such language the deaf-mute is unable to tell his own name or that of any of his friends, but he generally has signs for each by which he indicates them; and this sign is taken from prominent features in their appearance or action, viz., pointing to the place of the wedding ring for his mother, the whiskers for his father, and indicating the several heights for his brothers and sisters; limping to indicate some lame friend, and the sharpening of the knife for the butcher. It will thus be seen that the deaf-mute needs a language common to those around him by which he can communicate with the world. This is the greatest difficulty in deaf-mute instruction and requires years of toil, patience and perseverance. He learns everything through the eye, not by the ear. The first year at school is generally spent in teaching nouns and phrases and a little of arithmetic. The second year he goes over the same nouns and phrases and learn to combine words into sentences. Most intelligent deaf-mutes can write a few sentences to express their ideas, or write a short letter to their friends, after being two or three years at school.

The following is the uncorrected letter from a boy deaf and dumb from infancy after being three years in the Protestant (now Mackay) Institution for Deaf-mutes, at Montreal:—

DEAF MUTE EDUCATION.

"I received your very kind letter from you and was glad to hear from you and know that you are getting better now. My father told me will go to Montreal next September 3rd. I will be glad to see you and your family. I went to the mines last Tuesday. There was a man killed, he fell forty feet at the mines. The men are working the mines. It is rainy now. I am very busy. The crop is good, the plums is plenty. My cousin and me will mow the oats soon. I think you will go to New York one week. I am happy with my parents at home. I send my love to you."

The writer of this article received another letter from a converted Armenian Mohammedan who had been spending eight years at a college in the United States learning the English language. The Armenian understood and used his native language, for he was not deaf and dumb. We will compare his letter with that of the deaf-mute's. It will help to give some ideas of their difficulties in learning the English language. The Armenian had recently visited Montreal, and his impressions of the city and the people are curious:

"I am going Hamilton College, N. Y. Where am studying to return home Armenia, as I told you when your kind hospitality I was enjoying. I shook 3 times the dust of my foot just now against thise city, and again my brethren who herd me lest night in praree meating. I return my censer thank for loving kindness. 'I was a sturenger you took me in. The Lord give you helthe to teach blessed Gospele to those who are unable to hear yet Jesus Chrest dide for them for me and for aney body. Bible sed 'what me sow the same will me reap.' If I was verey rech the hall city would respect me. If I had nice dresses, stofepofe hat rengs on my fengers golden wach and chane and $. certainlly I could lechur on Koran and Mohammedanism. Brethen find plenety excuses just as faresees had when they sow the merecals which our Lord performe."

It is easy to teach a deaf-mute how to write, but a very different thing to get him to understand what he writes or what is written to him. Parents and teachers in public schools often make mistakes in attempting to teach little deaf and dumb children without any knowledge of the proper way. Once a schoolmaster brought a little deaf-mute boy to an institution for deaf-mutes in England, and said he had already taught him some useful knowledge. He was asked what he had taught him. He said he had taught him to know that "the way of the Lord was a good way." He was asked to show how he knew the boy understood the

sentence, and he made the boy copy it. This was to him sufficient proof, but he had never tried to explain to the boy either what God was, or what the way of God was. It would be a long time before a good teacher of deaf-mutes would bring such a sentence for his pupil to understand. He would explain to him something of the nature of the Almighty, when the pupil could understand the language necessary to express it, and then the way of God would still have to be explained as a metaphorical expression. To teach a deaf-mute an idea of a Supreme Being who is called " God," the teacher would begin thus : A desk is before the pupil. He asks him, " Who made it ?" " A man—a carpenter." " Of what is it made ?" " Of wood." " Did man make the wood ?" " No." " Where did he get it from ?" " Trees." " Did man make the trees ?" " No ; they grow." " How ?" " By the sun, rain, etc." " Does man make the sun shine and the rain to fall ?" " No." " Who does ?" They must be told that it is God who does all these things. So on step by step, from the works of man to the works of God, and from the creature to the Creator.

Lessons on secular subjects come in their turn—geography, history, arithmetic, etc.: but the great aim of the teacher is to give them a knowledge of ordinary language that they may understand what they read, and to be able to write down their thoughts for others not able to understand their signs and the finger language. Many of them do learn to write down their thoughts in correct language, and some of them learn to talk and read people's lips when they are spoken to orally.

DEAF MUTE EDUCATION.

CHAPTER IV.

ANECDOTES OF DEAF-MUTES.—A DEAF-MUTE'S PRAYER.—THE FINGER AND SIGN-LANGUAGE UTILIZED.—"JESUS AND ME."—DEAF-MUTE ARTISTS.—A PRODIGY.—DEAF-MUTE COMPOSITIONS.—MASSIEU AND CLERC—ABSURD EXPECTATIONS.

It would tire the reader to follow the deaf-mute through all the stages of his instruction at school, and it will perhaps be more pleasant to read a few anecdotes of deaf-mutes that have lived since the days of good Dr. Wallis and his early co-laborers.

About fifty years ago Lord Seaforth, who was born deaf and dumb, was to dine one day with Lord Melville in London. Just before the company arrived Lady Melville sent a lady who could talk on her fingers to meet Lord Seaforth and talk to him. Lord Guilford, who was not deaf and dumb, entered before Lord Seaforth, and the lady mistook him for the dumb lord, and entered into conversation with him on her fingers. He did the same. After a few minutes Lady Melville came into the room, and the lady said to her, " Well I have been talking away to this dumb man." " Dumb!" exclaimed Lord Guilford, " Bless me, I thought you were dumb!"

The following prayer was written by a deaf-mute boy named Joseph Turner of Edinburgh, who became a teacher of deaf-mutes, and was used by himself, because, as he said, he wanted to become a good man :

"O God, take pity on me ; bless me; forgive me my sin, for I am a poor guilty sinner; keep me from neglecting to think much of thee, and of Jesus Christ, and to pray to Thee. Give me wisdom of Thyself to think attentively how to pray to Thee. Oh! I thank Thee, for Thou hast given my master wisdom to teach me and my dear poor companions about the religion of Thee and of Jesus Christ. O ! pardon my sin; give me wisdom to understand surely what he says about religion. Oh! give me good care not to break the Sabbath day, but earnestly to read in the life of Christ. O God, open my mind surely to understand what I read in it. Oh! I would thank Thee to give my companions wisdom to understand what they read. Oh! hear me! Thou art God; besides Thee there is no Saviour. Thou art holy. Oh! make me to hate sin, and to love the good! Oh! give me grace to glorify Thee! Save me from hell; take me to Jesus Christ when I die. O Lord for the Sake of Christ, wilt Thou hear me? O God, give me good thoughts from heaven through Jesus Christ. I thank Thee that we are at peace in all the world, in Thy presence. Make us obedient to Thee and Jesus Christ Thy Son, in believing the gospel, and reading the Holy Bible concerning Thee and Him. O God, maker of heaven and earth, I look toward heaven. Forgive me my sin, for I have committed much against Thee and Thy dear Son Jesus Christ. Oh! I pray Thee, God, to be pitiful to me, a poor guilty sinner. Oh! my God into Thy hands I commit my soul. O God, accept me for Thine only Son's name's sake. O God, I am very thankful to Thee this morning for giving me health and sleep. Keep me from telling lies or bearing false witness against my dear poor companions this day. Oh! give them new hearts ; make them good, happy and wise, for they do not understand what Thou art. O Lord God, for the sake of Christ. Amen."

Many great men have found the manual alphabet of the deaf and dumb useful at different times. On one occasion an English judge,

DEAF MUTE EDUCATION.

while on one of his circuits, lost his way to the next assize town, and none of his party knew the road. A deaf and dumb woman came upon them at the two cross roads. The judge eagerly enquired of her the way to the town he was destined to hold assizes at, but she pointed to her ears and mouth and shook her head, to tell him that she was deaf and dumb, and did not understand him. The judge was in despair and turned to retrace his steps; but one of his party who had learned the alphabet of the deaf and dumb, spelled the name of the town to her, and she instantly pointed to the direction where the road led to the place. The judge gave her a shilling and rode on. He afterwards learned the alphabet himself, and soon found it useful in the trial of an unfortunate deaf-mute for robbery. He astonished all in the court by talking with the prisoner on his fingers and acting as interpreter for the lawyers.

The well-known authoress, Charlotte Elizabeth was quite deaf, like Dr. Kitto, the author of many valuable books on the Bible and Bible lands. Her husband became very expert in the use of the finger alphabet, and used to translate to her sermons and speeches in Parliament as quickly as they were delivered by the speakers.

Some years ago in a village church in Yorkshire, there might have been seen a very intelligent young girl interpreting the sermon to her deaf and dumb parents, between whom she sat during the service. The attention of the girl to the voice of the preacher, and the velocity with which she worked her fingers to convey to the eyes of her parents what she heard, excited great surprise in all who saw her for the first time thus employed.

The value of the deaf-mute alphabet to people not deaf and dumb has often been shown in different ways. We could write many interesting anecdotes illustrating the value of

> "That wondrous bridge, no bigger than the hand,
> By which truth travels to the silent land,"

had we time and space at our disposal. One more anecdote of the alphabet, and we will turn to something else.

Some years ago, a poor, homeless deaf and dumb girl in London was taken into service by a lady, and taught house-work. Her mistress learned the alphabet to communicate with her, and soon became expert in its use. Her husband, who was a banker, also learned it, and the girl became as easily to manage as if she were not deaf and dumb. One day the husband was obliged to bring to his home the treasures of the

bank on **account** of a **fire there.** This **came to the knowledge of a** burglar, who secreted **himself in the bed-room of the lady, where the** treasure was deposited. **The lady retired to bed** while the husband was absent on business. She **soon heard sneezing under the** bed, but remained quiet, **as** if asleep. **The burglar then emerged from** his hiding-place and demanded of the **lady to** know where the **money** was deposited. **She was** terrified **at his** threats and referred him to an iron safe in a **corner.** While he was trying to open it he heard the footsteps **of the** husband ascending the **stairs,** and he rushed to his former hiding place, threatening the lady with **instant** death if she said a word about him or left the room. The husband **noticed** his wife's paleness and asked her what was the matter. She answered aloud, " I have a bad headache," and immediately spelled on her fingers, " Hush, there is a burglar under the bed." The husband answered, " My dear, I am sorry for your headache ; you must have a cup of tea," and thrust the poker into the fire, saying it was a cold night. When the poker was red hot, he turned to the servant man who had come into the room, **and** said, " Thomas, there is a man under the bed. Do you think this **poker** will bring him out ?" The burglar at once left his hiding place and begged for mercy. " How did you know I was here ?" he said. " The **lady did not** tell you, I know she did not speak one word about **me.**" **He** was given into custody and afterwards sent over the seas to a distant penal settlement, and never knew how his presence under the bed was revealed to the gentleman. The gentleman became a very warm friend to deaf-mutes and their schools ever afterwards.

The sign language of the deaf and dumb in **the** hands of an experienced **teacher** often shows its vast importance in trying circumstances. One anecdote which came to the knowledge of the writer will sufficiently illustrate **this:** A few years ago the London police found a deaf and dumb woman, totally uneducated, wandering about the streets at midnight. She could give no account of herself, and the police kindly took her to **the** workhouse near by for safe keeping. Every effort of the officers **of the** workhouse to discover her name and residence failed. A missionary **to** the deaf and dumb was sent for to try to find out from where she had come. He found she was utterly ignorant of the alphabet, nor could she read or write. He soon found by her signs that she had been brought by railway to London by a man with whiskers and then deserted. Now, as no signs could discover her name and residence, the missionary was **in a** difficulty. He, however, **did** not give her case up

DEAF MUTE EDUCATION.

as hopeless, but hired a cab and told the driver to drive wherever she might direct. She directed them on up one street and down another till they came to the London Bridge Station. The missionary asked her in signs if they were to get out. She shook her head to say "No." On they went till they came to the steamboat landing. She then told him to stop and get out. The sight of the steamboat gave her great pleasure, and the missionary understood by her signs that she was to go on board one of the steamers, and pointed towards Lambeth. Tickets were bought for that place, and on arrival there the young woman was overjoyed, and jumped out of the boat, making eager signs to her kind friend to follow. They then hastened on foot through several streets, the young woman acting as guide, till they came to a house, which she entered. A ticket was in the window with "This House to Let" on it, which the missionary read with some misgiving, and presently the young woman returned with a sad countenance, signing to the missionary that her parents or friends had gone away! The missionary made enquiries of the neighbours, and they informed him that the occupants of the house had left a few days ago, and gone to another part of London. He obtained their names and the address to which they had removed, and soon found the girl's parents, who were overwhelmed with joy at the recovery of their poor daughter, whom they said had been decoyed away by a bad man.

Deaf mutes sometimes make funny sentences in trying to learn the English language. At one school a little deaf-mute boy was asked to show his skill in the use of the English language on his slate, and he wrote: "A man ran from a cow. He is a coward." He thus unconsciously perpetrated a pun, which caused the visitors great amusement.

A few years ago, an English lady was teaching a school for hearing children in Demerara; and a colored deaf and dumb girl came to learn to read and write. The missionary's wife and the teacher shook their heads, and thought that it was impossible, and signed for her to go home. Day by day she came to the school and would not be refused. At last the teacher wrote to England for the deaf and dumb alphabet. It was surprising how quickly the poor girl learned the English language. By-and-bye she could read the New Testament, from which she learned to love Jesus as her Saviour. One day she wrote to her kind teacher, "Missie, me too happy. You would think when me walk out that there were two peoples in the road, but it is *Jesus and me*. He talk and me talk, and we are two too happy together."

DEAF MUTE EDUCATION.

A deaf and dumb pupil of the great French landscape painter Corot (who died in 1875), got from his master a paper on which was written "Conscience," which so impressed the deaf-mute that in copying one of his beautiful pencil drawing he even tried to imitate a stain of glue. Corot, when he saw it, smiled, and wrote to him: "Very well, my friend; but when you are before Nature you will not see any stains."

In speaking of deaf-mute artists, I would like to tell an anecdote of the Scotch deaf-mute artist. Walter Geikie, whose interesting biography was written by the late Sir T. D. Lauder, Bart. Geikie was a very clever artist, and has left many much-prized drawings. He died in 1838. An anecdote regarding an individual who makes a very conspicuous appearance among the characters found in his etchings, is worth relating as an example of the difficulties he encountered in his ardent desire to collect the portraits of people who he saw in the streets of Edinburgh. The porter of the Grassmarket was a singular character and arrested Geikie's attention. He was somewhat pot-bellied, and with that projection and hang of the nether lip, and elevation of nose that give to the human countance a certain air of vulgar importance. In this subject it seemed to say: "Though I'm a porter, I'm no fool." Geikie had made several attempts to get near enough to sketch this man. Day after day he hunted his intended victims with pencil and sketch-book, but failed to get a chance of him. The porter perceived him, and suspecting his intention, at once moved on and plunged into the crowd. Like a young Highland sportsman, who wishes to get a shot at an old fox who may have dodged into cover, Geikie, with pencil and paper in hand, prowled about after his prey. But the porter was on his guard and took good care to keep behind other people, so as to defy the attempts of the young artist, until at last, when the market began to thin, and his hopes of defeating the foul intention against him ebbed away with the lessening crowd, he lost all patience, and abused and threatened his tormenter with great fury, both of words and actions. The first were of course lost upon the poor deaf lad, although there was no mistaking the meaning shake of the porter's mutton fist. But as this only threw his subject into a more tempting attitude, the artist's fervor for his art rendered him utterly regardless of consequences, and he tried his pencil with great enthusiasm! This enraged the porter, who roared like an infuriated bull, and rushed at Geikie to punish him for his boldness; and before Geikie had time to apply his pencil to the

paper, he was obliged to fly to save his bones. The porter's heavy weight prevented anything like an equal race, so Geikie kept ahead and made rapid sketches of his approaching foe at every stop he made, as they ran up the Grassmarket. The porter was all the time puffing and blowing and labouring after him, and his fury seemed to be increased at every step. He made use of every nerve to catch the young artist, which prevented him making further use of his pencil. Fortunately an open stair of one of the large buildings most opportunely presented itself, into which Geikie rushed, and the porter remained outside watching for the return of his enemy. He stood outside with his hands under the tails of his coat. Geikie had a capital view of him from one of the windows, and immediately set to work with his pencil and executed an admirable sketch of one of the most curious men of Edinburgh, who has long since passed away. When the sketch was executed Geikie found that the porter kept watch for him, so he had to remain in his hiding place for several hours. When, at last, the porter got tired of keeping sentry and moved away, Geikie emerged from his retreat, went home, and saw him no more. In the collection of this clever deaf artist the reader will find the remarkable character above described in the plate entitled "Street Auctioneer," and he is in the act of consulting his old-fashioned chronometer.

Many more interesting and amusing anecdotes could be told of deaf-mute artists (for there are many of them in England), and of deaf-mutes in various other professions, but space is limited. Sometimes deaf-mutes display great intelligence and attain to a respectable niche of fame in art, science and literature. We will mention one instance of the extraordinary calibre of a congenial deaf-mute—a prodigy. Some years ago a benevolent gentleman found a red-headed, ragged little deaf-mute in the streets of Glasgow, and took him to the school for deaf-mutes in that city. He showed considerable intelligence, and the gentleman thought he was a rough diamond but capable of being highly polished by education and training. During the first session at school the boy shot ahead of every other pupil, and there were then more than a hundred, many of them having been there for seven or eight years. The rapidity with which he learned was amazing; indeed his memory was so retentive that what he once read he never forgot. Such was the calibre of his mind that nothing was too difficult for his comprehension. He reads books on mathematics, metaphysics and the like, whether they were printed in English, foreign or dead languages, which

he also **read with ease.** When school was over, he would rush to the library, **take out a lot** of books under his arms, and **make** his way to the nearest **fire to** read **them,** while his school-mates **directed** their steps to the play-ground. Such was the force of habit **that he** would sit near the **fire even** during summer while he studied. **No wonder with** a mind **so** well stored with knowledge, he **was a** capital story-teller. **He** never used signs since the day he could spell on his fingers. He was **appointed an** assistant-teacher at school, but he found the task too **irksome, and left the** institution to become a common labourer in order **to make money more** rapidly to purchase books. **He** spent all his money in **books** and neglected his bodily wants. His **books** increased in number very fast, and they formed his table, chair **and** bed, by being piled one upon another in his lodgings. They **were** his only articles **of** furniture. The extraordinary learning of this deaf and dumb laborer **attracted** the attention of many gentlemen and his employers, who thought that he was not in his proper sphere. They determined to give him a better position so that his fund of knowledge might **be** put **to** some use. They visited his lodgings for **this** purpose one day **when** he was not at work, and **found** him dead **on his** bed **of** books, **having** literally starved his body **to** death to feed **his** hungry mind. **He had** everything ready for writing **a** book, which **he said** would astonish **the** world. There were **several** reams of paper **and a** large bottle **of ink,** showing that he fully **intended to enter upon the** work, but there was no indication of what **work** it would **be. His** stock of books were printed in several languages of the highest **kind of** literature. **He** was sixteen or eighteen years **old** when he died. He had **a** florid countenance, red hair, greenish eyes inclining **to** blue, which gave him a peculiar expression.

The following is an extract from a deaf-mute's letter to his teacher in Glasgow, Dr. Anderson :

"**How** graceful indeed is the very idea of placing some tangible **token of** our gratitude in **the** hands of our old teacher whilst bidding him **welcome to** the repose **which** he so greatly desiderates in the evening **of his** arduous life! For **I** firmly maintain that a simple address, however **pregnant with** the affecting pathos of a myriad of hearts overflowing with **gratitude,** such as that with which Dr. Peet was presented by his old pupils last year, would not do sufficient justice to our own real sentiments **nor to** our benefactor's merits."

Another writes in the following strain respecting the education of **deaf-mutes,** which contains much **truth :**

DEAF MUTE EDUCATION.

"The deaf-mute on leaving school, is a changed being, quite different from what he was before he went there; he is now so intelligent that he may resort to the society of the wise and good, maintain proper conduct towards his neighbors, and even hold an intercourse with that Being to whom he owes his life, with every enjoyment that can render life easy and comfortable. Under the circumstances, the education of the deaf and dumb must be among the most extraordinary and remarkable instances of philanthrophy in modern times."

The above are specimen of British deaf-mute composition which surpass anything ever penned by the famous deaf-mutes of the past century—Massieu, Clerc and many others. Who has not read the brillant metaphorical sayings of the impracticable Massieu, the famous pupil of Abbe Sicard? Respecting whom Dr. Buxton, Principal of the Liverpool Institution for Deaf-mutes, says: "His best replies were short, terse, pointed, and metaphorical withal. These are all characteristics of the Abbe Sicard's style, both in his writings and in his speeches; but if they are the natural characteristics of any deaf man's diction, I have been singularly unfortunate, for I have never found it so. If there is one thing they cannot do, and rarely learn to do, and never excel in doing, it is the use of metaphors." Yet among Massieu's sayings are these. —" Hope is the flower of happiness," " Indifference is the neutrality of the soul," " Judgment is the interior sight of the mind," " Reason is the torch of the mind, judgment is its guide," " Prudence is the Minerva of the soul, and rules our words and actions," " Enemy is the intellectual viper which gnaws the heart and envenoms it," " Jealousy is a serpent without venom," etc.

It is now well known that the questions and answers attributed to Massieu were committed to memory, and formed part of the system of teaching by Abbe Sicard. Massieu was, according to his friend and school-mate, Clerc, extremely foolish. "His childishness and vanity, his absurd follies and oddities of conduct were so extravagent as sometimes to disgust even those who worked with him, and were taught by him. His love of finery was as ridiculous as that of Oliver Goldsmith; and it might have been as truly said of him, as it was of Charles II.—

"He never said a foolish thing,
And never did a wise one."

It was his brilliant sayings alone which made him famous, but they have done more harm than good. They were delusive and led people

DEAF MUTE EDUCATION.

to expect every deaf-mute taught in the Institution to be able to utter similar grandiloquent sentences, and to do readily and spontaneously what they can scarcely do at all. Even in our own time the fame of Massieu continues to deceive and mislead. It leads to disappointment on all sides. Parents are disappointed, subscribers are disappointed, the pupils are disappointed, the reputation and possibly the funds of the Institution suffer and the whole blame falls upon the unfortunate teacher because he is not Sicard, and cannot turn out, not one Massieu, but a score or a hundred.

When the Rev. T. H. Gallaudet went from America to Europe, in 1815, to seek knowledge and experience before he entered upon his work of deaf-mute instruction in the Western World, he found Massieu and Clerc in the full vigour of their powers, and at the height of their fame. He first visited England without finding what he sought, and went away disappointed to France. He was, in fact, compelled to decide upon his course, and make his choice at Paris. Whom, then, did he select as his co-worker and life companion? Not Massieu, but Clerc. Not the repeater of sparkling answers, but the practical, solid, working teacher. His whole life shows that the founder of the American Asylum was a man of great sagacity. The late Dr. Peet, President of the New York Institution, in the published report of his visit to the various schools for the deaf and dumb in Europe, in 1841, says, respecting Massieu—" Even Massieu, whose fame a few brilliant answers given at public exercises have spread through the world, was after testimony of those who knew him best, unable to write a page in correct French, or to follow out to any length a consecutive chain of reasoning." Then after citing Clerc, by way of contrast, and as showing what a pupil of rare talent may become, in spite of the defects of the system under which he was trained, Dr. Peet finishes the paragraph by saying, " Such is the prevalent judgment passed upon Sicard in Paris; I only repeat it." (Report on European Institutions, page 98.)

In speaking of the disappointment caused by the brilliant answers of Massieu, an anecdotes recorded in Dr. Orpen's work, " Anecdotes of the Deaf and Dumb," may here be introduced and read by any one with profit, as it shows the absurd expectations as to the progress of deaf-mute children entertained by persons who forget the excessive difficulty of their instruction. Rev. J. D. Hastings, speaking at the tenth annual meeting of the Deaf and Dumb Institution, Dublin, said: "I wish to mention one fact which came under my notice. I happened to be at the

Institution on a visiting day; there were several persons present at the time; among the number was a lady and her son, with whom I had the honour to be acquainted; the lady is now within the hearing of my voice; she asked one of the little girls, I believe, the smallest in the school (Cecilia White), a question; she had it written on the slate; it was, 'Do you remember the first promise of the Messiah?' The children looked and looked again, and then made a sign to know what was Messiah; the lady wrote on the slate, 'the Anointed or Sent.' The little girl looked again, then looked at me, and made a sign, by pointing to her head, to say she did not know. The lady turned to me and said, 'Now I am convinced the Bible is not taught in the school; I was informed before of this, but I determined on judging for myself.' I endeavored to show her that it was quite unreasonable to expect a child, who was deaf and dumb, to have that knowledge which other children possess. I found all was in vain. I then said to her, 'Perhaps you would permit me to ask your son (who to all appearance was three or four years older than the little girl), a similiar question.' The lady at once assented. I asked him could he tell me, 'What was the second promise of the Messiah?' After some time I looked for an answer; but no, the boy was as dumb as the little girl. His mamma looked at him, but no answer. At length I said, 'Perhaps the question is too difficulty; but I will be satisfied if you remove the odium from the dumb girl, and consequently from the Institution; tell me, 'What was the first promise of the Messiah?' No answer, he could not tell. In vain the mamma looked with anxious eye; but alas! no reply. The lady said, 'Answer the question, my dear.' Indeed, mamma, said he, 'I cannot.' Thus was the Institution brought into disgrace; while a boy three or four years older and possessed of those faculties which had been denied to this poor girl, was unable to answer the question. I thanked the little boy, and said, 'I would not say that he did not read his Bible, nor would I say to the lady that it was not taught in his family; but I would say the question was beyond his comprehension.' After some further examination of the little girl, the lady was quite satisfied that the Bible taught in the school; and I am happy to say, sir, that we have not only was that lady's guinea, but her good wishes, with a determination to forward the views of the Institution so far as she possibly can."

CHAPTER V.

THE SYSTEMS OF INSTRUCTION.

There are three systems employed in teaching deaf-mutes, viz.:— The *Mechanical Articulation Method*, which is the oldest of all systems, was invented by Heinicke, a Saxon, about the year 1750. This system aims at developing the powers of speech, and the educating of the eye of the pupil to perform as far as it can the part of the ear. This system is now generally assisted by Visible Speech, invented by Professor A. Graham Bell, late of London, England, and now of Washington, U.S. It is now employed in most institutions for deaf-mutes. For semi-mutes, or those who have learned to speak before becoming deaf, this method is the best.

The *Natural Method*, or the language of pantomime. This system was founded by Abbe L'Epee, of Paris, and is employed chiefly in the United States and France. By this method signs are used at every stage of the pupils' instruction, and is often carried to excess in many schools, preventing the pupils from acquiring a good command of their native language. For imparting religious instruction, lecturing and communicating with uneducated deaf-mutes this method is exceedingly convenient.

The *Combined Method* is a system of instruction embracing the first and second methods which, we believe, was first used by Thomas Braidwood in London. In schools employing this system the teachers recognize the utility of the sign-language, and use articulation where practicable. This system enables the teacher to teach deaf mutes of all degrees of intellect and none are turned away without deriving more or less benefit from it. It calls to the aid of the teacher every new or old plan which may have been found to be beneficial or of value in imparting instruction to either the congenital deaf-mute or the semi-mute. The *combined method* is employed in all the large institutions in Europe and America, and is growing more and more popular every year.

CHAPTER VI.

THE MENTAL AND MORAL **CONDITION OF THE** UNEDUCATED DEAF-MUTES.—NO **IDEAS** OF A CREATOR.—IS **CONSCIENCE PRIMITIVE?**

We have frequently been asked for information respecting the deaf-mute's ideas of God and the soul previous to his instruction. This subject has often been discussed by learned men. The testimonies of deaf-mutes themselves are substantially alike, as to their having had no idea of the Creator before instruction.

To the twenty-second report of the American Asylum are annexed several questions, addressed to a number of pupils, whose average age on joining the school was about fourteen. "Before you were instructed in the Asylum had you any idea of the Creator?" The answers, substantially alike, are given by thirteen pupils. "No, I did not know that a Creator existed. I had no idea of God before I entered the Asylum." "Had you reasoned or thought about the world, or the beings and things it contains?" "I never attempted to suppose who had made the world, or how it had ever come into existence." "Had you any idea of your own soul?" "I never conceived such a thing as a soul, nor was I ever conscious that my mind had faculties and operations different and distant from those of my body." Their answers shows how little their friends at home had been able to teach them.

The mental and moral condition of the uneducated deaf-mute has been found to be so low that men of science and education have asked "Is conscience primitive?"

It was only recently that our attention was called to an article on this subject in the Popular Science Monthly by the editor of the Canadian Illustrated News, who requested our views on the matter. There seems to be much ground for the belief that conscience is not primitive in the congenital deaf-mute before instruction. We have, after nearly twenty years experience as a teacher of deaf-mutes and from personal experience, been led to believe that "conscience" as now understood—the internal self-knowledge or judgment of right and wrong, the knowledge of our own actions as well as those of others—is an acquired faculty in the deaf-mute. We possess no record of a congenital deaf-mute who, by his own unaided efforts, has found the being of a God, or discovered the fact of his own immortality. His mind is indeed dark and inert—in fact, hermetically sealed. How could it be otherwise in

DEAF MUTE EDUCATION.

his condition? Locke says that man has no innate ideas, but that his mind in early infancy is like a blank sheet of paper, ready to receive any external impressions. So with the uneducated deaf-mute. His mind remains a blank so long as he is uninstructed. The famous Abbe Sicard, of Paris, a world-renowned teacher of deaf-mutes, says that "a deaf-mute (congenital and uninstructed) is a perfect cipher, a living automaton. He possesses not the sure instinct by which the animal creation is guided. He is alone in nature, with no possible exercise of his intellectual faculties which remain without action." Sicard, however, refers to the deaf-mutes of his day, nearly a hundred years ago, when through neglect, and being hidden from society as a family disgrace, the germs of the rational and moral faculties were scarcely manifested. Such treatment of deaf-mutes in our own time is rare, and, with kindness and sympathy from the beginning, their minds have received considerable development. If conscience means internal self-knowledge, or judgment of right and wrong, a mind so dark, so inert, and wholly uninstructed as that of the uneducated congenital deaf-mute, could not reasonably be expected to possess anything like it. Uneducated deaf-mutes seldom exhibit compunctions of conscience when they have done anything wrong, but such symptoms gradually appear as they grow older and some instruction is imparted. The testimony of educated deaf-mutes themselves goes to support this view, and the personal experience and observation of the writer confirms it to a great extent.

Their moral and intellectual condition before instruction is little above that of the more intelligent brutes, and lower than that of the most unenlightened savages. All philologists and mental philosophers agree that it is the gift of language that chiefly distinguishes man from the brutes, and that without it he would have little claim to the title of a rational being. The testimony of educated deaf-mutes throws much light upon the amount of knowledge they possessed before coming under systematic instruction. Very few of them had any idea of the creation of the world, or of the plants and animals which it contains. Their own reflections, and all the imperfect attempts of their friends to instruct them, have failed to give them any idea of the existence of a God or the soul. We need not wonder at this when we read that Ovid, who lived in the learned and polished era of Augustus, expressed the popular belief of his time in the theory that all things were produced by the due union of heat and moisture, which shows that deaf-mutes have not been alone in the utter ignorance of the existence of a Creator. The existence

of the soul after death has never occurred to the uneducated mute. All the efforts of anxious parents to convey some idea to this end have failed. The pointing to the fire to convey an idea of hell impresses the mute that the body will be thrown into a fire for some cause by some person at some indefinite time. Before receiving instruction the writer, whose home was within sight of the parish church and the county jail, had his notions of heaven and hell formed by his mother always pointing to one or to the other of those buildings according to the nature of his conduct or actions. If he required reproof she would point to the jail and fire, but if she wished to show that she was pleased with his behaviour she would pat his head and point to the church, and then upwards and assume a reverent look. From this mode of control he formed his idea that the church was the place for those who had fine clothes and were well behaved, and that the minister was the object of worship or admiration. The jail he thought was for the poor, the drunkard, and those that robbed orchards, who were there cast bodily into a fire. Having observed a man in the street whom he once saw taken into a jail, his astonishment was very great on finding that neither the man's person nor his clothes had been burned. The next time his mother threatened him with the terrors of the jail and the fire for misconduct, he gazed at her with a look of incredulity, shook his head and laughed. Queer ideas about death have been entertained by uneducated deaf-mutes. Most of them have thought that death was only sleep, and to put a body in a coffin and bury it seemed to them to be an act of cruelty. They have no sense of moral wrong-doing. They think they ought to be allowed to do just as they please, no matter what it may be. A most intelligent lady, a congenital mute, who had reached a nature age before receiving any systematic instruction, confessed that she had been practicing falsehood for many years without the slightest notion that she was doing wrong. This is not an uncommon fault with this class of people. Another of great intelligence had been in the habit of falsehood and dishonesty without any compunctions of conscience. He never dreamed that he was doing wrong, and only dreaded the punishment which followed detection. Many instances could be cited if necessary from deaf-mute testimony in support of the assertion that the uneducated deaf-mute has no moral sense of right and wrong. He is a practical atheist, and if his friends have tried to give him an idea of a Supreme Power and such takes root in his mind, his conceptions on the point are most vague and unsatisfactory. Teachers of deaf-mutes have frequently

DEAF MUTE EDUCATION.

watched the gradual development of the mind of their new pupils. It is found that, by associating among the other pupils, the new arrivals will soon gain the idea of a Being existing above "who can see them, and is angry when they behave badly," and the pointing upwards is often used by one pupil as a check upon another who is inclined to be naughty. Sometimes it has this effect, but we have more than once seen the admonitions defied by young deaf-mutes who have not yet obtained clear ideas on the subject. We have seen them disputing and their antagonistic principles aroused when one has been desirious of saying something especially annoying to his opponent, who, he knows, has a reverence for the Being above, and is shocked when anything is said against Him. He will say in his signs "God-bad," not knowing his blasphemy, yet with a secret shrug that he has gained his point, beaten his antagonist, who rushes with horror expressed on his countenance to report to his teacher the profanity of the other.

When the deaf-mute is put under careful control he comes to associate in his mind a line of conduct with what produces pain, and another line of conduct with what produce pleasure. Out of this grows a sort of conscience which leads him to be sorrowful when he does certain things, and to be glad when he does the contrary. This conscience is entirely dependent upon the person to whom he is subjected. "Given a good master," says Dr. Peet, the highest authority in America, "and he will be very likely to have a kind of moral sense that will be a safe guide in the life he leads, and will bring about habits that will be useful to him hereafter." So quite the reverse will be his conduct if he be placed under a bad master. He may be obedient, diligent, affectionate, habitually honest, but it will be owing to the influence of kind and firm control and good example—not to the higher moral and religious motives that are addressed to children who hear. He is too often self-willed, passionate, prone to secret vice and suspicious, but these bad qualities are generally the outcome of parental indulgence, and in having been the butt of thoughtless young people.

Is the uneducated deaf-mute morally and legally responsible? is a question which has been often discussed. In many criminal cases, both in Europe and America, uneducated deaf-mutes have frequently figured for murder, but they have been treated as irresponsible beings, and no sentence has been passed on them.

There can be no more pitiable object than an uneducated deaf-mute, except where blindness is added to that of deafness. His condition

points to conclusions which cannot be evaded. It is the duty of society to provide for his instruction at the proper age, and it is criminal on the part of parents and guardians who neglect to secure for their unfortunate child the benefits within their reach. To the deaf-mute education means everything. It means intercourse with fellow-men, hope, happiness, the pleasant communion with the highest intellectual achievements of men of all countries and all ages, which we find in books. It makes life in this world enjoyable and gives him hope of salvation in the world to come. To deny the deaf-mute education is to keep his mind on a level with the brutes. "To the hearing child," says Dr. Peet, "every word spoken in his presence is a means of intellectual development. Every person, literate or illiterate, with whom he comes in contact is for the time his conscious or unconscious teacher. In fact school gives him so small a portion of the knowledge he possesses that it may be considered rather the regulator than the source of his attainments. To the deaf-mute it means home, happiness; it means the full and free exercise of all the rights, immunities and privileges which belong to humanity."

DEAF MUTE EDUCATION.

CHAPTER VII.

MARRIAGES AMONG DEAF-MUTES.

We will now consider *the marriage of the deaf and dumb with each other* We have known people to declare that such unions are very wicked, and ought not to be allowed: but their opinion is mainly founded on the belief that this intermarriage invariably perpetuates the infirmity, which is quite a mistake. We admit that the children of deaf and dumb parents are occasionally similarly afflicted, but the cases are rare—they are quite the exception. In London we know of 114 instances of this kind of union; 76 marriages have had offspring, but in only seven of these instances is the offspring deaf and dumb, and in these cases one or more of the brothers or sisters of one of the parents have been so afflicted. On the other hand, we know of deaf and dumb parents who have had as many as nine children, not one of which was deaf; we have known, on the contrary, cases where both parents have had all their faculties, but out of ten children five have been deaf and dumb; and the report of the London Asylum gives an instance where out of ten children eight were deaf and dumb. This argument, therefore, of perpetuating deafness, though it may be thus applied in the least degree, is not, says the Rev. S. Smith, chaplain of the Royal Association in Aid of the Deaf and Dumb, London, strong enough to support any one in prohibiting such marriages as wicked, when other facts are taken into consideration; for since it is shown that it is in quite exceptional cases that the offspring of these intermarriages inherit the same infirmity, it will not be denied that deaf-mutes have a right to marry as well as other persons, and whom they ought to marry depends upon each one's choice and acceptance. Now it will readily be granted that there will be the most sympathy and love between persons whose feelings, tastes, and habits offer a certain resemblance, and who can communicate freely with each other. Comparatively few hearing people know the deaf and dumb language, and a very small proportion of those who do would marry a deaf and dumb person, unless some advantage were connected with the union: indeed it may be that in the whole of a deaf and dumb man's hearing acquaintances not one eligible female knows his language; it is evident therefore that he will generally seek a wife amongst those of his own class, and in London, the instances existing and known to us where this intermarriage has taken place stand in the proportion of four to one

where the woman can hear. Again, not many hearing men would marry a deaf and dumb woman without a consideration as a "make-weight." Only four cases of this kind are known to us in London. Besides, we have been told by very respectable deaf and dumb females that they would not have confidence in him; he would not take the trouble to tell them everything; perhaps he would have hearing friends come to see him, and then they would be shut out from the general conversation; they would prefer one like themselves—one who had no advantages over them. We argue, nevertheless, that the best wife for a deaf and dumb man—if he can find one and persuade her to marry him—is a woman who can hear, one who has acquired a ready means of communication with him, sympathizes with his affliction, and so is prepared to take upon herself a larger share than ordinary of the management of their family and joint affairs, which must devolve upon her on account of her husband's deprivation; and the higher and best educated class, as a rule, do obtain this kind of wife; their eyes are open to the advantages of such a help-meet. As one of them has written: "When a man marries, he ought to try and supply that wherein he is deficient; a deaf and dumb man wants some one to hear and speak for him. A deaf man taking a deaf woman to be his companion would find the various hindrances which he meets in his daily life doubled and increased; he would be obliged to go to some one else than his wife to interpret or to explain for him." The hearing sisters or daughters of deaf and dumb persons would be most likely to fulfil the necessary requirements; and it so happens that the hearing wife of one deaf-mute gentleman, who is much praised by her husband, had a brother similarly afflicted, of whom she was very fond; but death snatching him away from her love, she took the opportunity of supplying his place by a husband from the same class, and an excellent wife she has proved. We also know other similar cases with the same happy result. But, returning to the general rule prevalent amongst them of intermarriage amongst themselves, we can bear testimony that when two are well-matched, intelligent, and of amiable disposition, and especially if they act from Christian principle, they get on together exceedingly well. There is, however, some disadvantage as regards their children; they cannot receive early instruction in spoken language and moral training: they may learn vulgar expressions from other children, and use them toward each other in their parents' presence without their cognizance, and in this they are unable to correct them. Some of these disadvant-

DEAF MUTE EDUCATION.

ages are, however, soon overcome by an early attendance at school. The children of the deaf and dumb soon learn to communicate with their parents by signs, and it is very amusing to see little things two or three years old beginning thus to make known their wants to them. So that, taking all these circumstances into consideration, we may consistently state that deaf-mute intermarriages are not advisable in those cases where a suitable hearing partner can be obtained, but they are not wicked, nor are they to be prohibited, lest a worse thing come to pass. Still this precaution should be taken by the deaf and dumb, not to choose those in whose families any hereditary tendency has manifested itself.

In Canada and the United States there are many deaf-mute unions. Perhaps no country in the world shows so many deaf-mute intermarriages as does the latter country, and many of them have produced deaf-mute children, but it has not been found necessary to prohibit or discourage them on that account. There are about a dozen deaf-mute married couples in the Dominion of Canada, and most of them have families, but none, as far as we have been able to learn, have deaf-mute children.

DEAF MUTE EDUCATION.

LAURA BRIDGMAN.

DEAF MUTE EDUCATION.

CHAPTER VIII.

BLIND DEAF-MUTES.—LAURA BRIDGMAN.—MARY BRADLEY.—JOSEPH **HAGUE.—ANEC**DOTES.—DEATH OF HAGUE.—OTHER CASES ON RECORD.

There are, happily, **but few** human beings **who in addition to the loss** of hearing are also **deprived** of sight, and are therefore at **once deaf, dumb,** and blind. These appear **to** be so entirely cut off from **the** outer **world that** the position seems **at** first sight beyond **the** reach of amelioration; **and** was until a comparatively recent **date** believed to be so, even by those whose ingenuity was daily taxed to find means **to** reach the minds of those who are deprived of hearing only.

The case of a **deaf,** dumb, and blind youth, the son of a Scotch minister, attracted a large amount of attention early in the last century. Curiosity **was excited to** watch the habits **of** the youth, in **order** to see whether **there** was not some loophole by which light might be made to penetrate the darkness **within,** but nothing could be devised which yielded any **result.**

It **was not until the** wonderful revelation of the **case** of Laura Bridgman **by the late Charles Dickens was made in his "** American Notes " in 1842-3, **that** attention **was** again **awakened to the** consideration of blind deaf-mutes, and the possibility **of reaching and** developing **a mind so** completely isolated. **The** statement **made by** Mr. Dickens were of so extraordinary a **character** that few persons—especially those engaged in educating **the** deaf **and** dumb—could give them credence, **and many** persons concluded that he must have been imposed upon, or that the narrative was only " the tale of a traveller," related to astonish **and amuse.** Since she first **appeared in the pages** of Dickens, over **40 years ago,** Laura Bridgman has been the theme of many articles in magazines and reviews, and the subject of countless allusions. The most recent account of her remarkable case appears in the American Magazine **for June, 1887.** As it gives the latest known details **of** the life of this now historical woman we here insert the article entire:—

" **Perhaps some** younger readers have **never** heard of Laura Dewey Bridgman. **It was just** half a century ago **when she, a child** of seven years' age, **began** to receive an education at **a** Boston asylum for the blind. The method of that instruction and **its great** success are among **the** marvels **of our** civilization; they attracted profound attention and study for **many years; led to great** improvements in the art of teaching

DEAF MUTE EDUCATION.

deaf-mutes, and paved the way for a clearer insight into the constitution of man.

"For every care, for every expenditure lavished upon such unfortunates, mankind has been ten thousand times rewarded; it was in the endeavor to help deaf-mutes that Alexander Graham Bell invented the telephone.

Laura Bridgman's case the sense of feeling was the only avenue by which knowledge could enter the mind. She had totally lost the senses of sight, hearing and smell; that of taste was so much impaired that she recognized no difference between rhubarb and strong tea. She had lost the very memory of these senses, with their destruction by scarlet fever when she was two years old; the power of articulate speech was gone, and in her ninth year even the capacity to distinguish between bright light and darkness had wholly ceased.

"Her instructor, Dr. S. G. Howe, says in 1838:

"'Her mind dwells in darkness and stillness as profound as that of a closed tomb at midnight. Of beautiful sights and sweet sounds and pleasant odors she had no conception. Nevertheless she seems as happy and playful as a bird or lamb, and the employment of her intellectual faculties or acquirement of a new idea, gives her a vivid pleasure which is plainly marked in her expressive features. She never seems to repine, but has all the buoyancy and gaiety of childhood. She is fond of fun and frolic, and when playing with the rest of the children her laugh sound loudest of the group.'

"Her intellectual powers had not been touched by the disease that destroyed most of her senses. But to reach her mind and develope her thoughts seemed an almost hopeless task. Dr. Howe quotes from Blackstone:

"'A man who is born deaf, dumb and blind is looked upon by the law as in the same state as an idiot; he being supposed incapable of of any understanding, as wanting all those senses which furnish the human mind with ideas.'

"But in Laura's case, after the early difficulties were overcome, it was found that she was as anxious to learn as her instructors were to teach. Many years elapsed before the final stages of this instruction were attained. But the first, and as if intuitively, Miss Laura was a stickler for the proprieties of life. Even when she was in the flush of her girlish fame, and both conscious and proud of the interest she elicited, Laura made *gentlemen* visitors keep their distance. Ladies

DEAF MUTE EDUCATION.

could fondle her and sometimes take her in their laps; the male was fortunate who got even a few minutes' converse through an interpreting teacher, a mere handshake being ordinarily sufficient. Still more curious, not to say inexplicable, were her distinct and correct notions of morality; a knowledge that it was wrong to lie or steal before she had been taught anything whatever about truthfulness or the rights of others.

"The story of Laura Dewey **Bridgman's** education has been often told. It was for many years the theme of numerous discussions, that extended over a wide range. For instance, Calvinistic theologians were asked what would become of her soul if Laura should die before receiving any knowledge of what dying meant; without any conception of a soul, a future, a God; and yet with a keen and active intelligence and a conscience that distinguish between right and wrong.

"**The teaching** began by impressing upon her mind a connection between an object and its name in print. Dr. Howe had previously affixed labels to various common objects, such as knife, fork, spoon, key, chair and stove; the labels were printed in the raised letters used by the blind.

"'First we gave her the word "knife" on a slip of paper, and moved her fingers over it as the blind do in reading. Then we showed her the knife, and let her feel the label upon it, and made to her the sign which she was accustomed to use to signify likeness, viz.: placing side by side the forefingers of each hand. She readily perceived the similarity of the two words.

"'The same process was repeated with other articles. This exercise lasted three-quarters of an hour. She received from it only the idea that some of the labels were alike, others unlike. The lesson was repeated in the afternoon, and on the next day. About the third day she began to comprehend that the words on the slips of paper represented the objects on which they were pasted. This was shown by her taking the word "chair" and placing it first upon one chair and then upon another, while a smile of intelligence lighted her hitherto puzzled countenance.'

"**After thus** learning several words, and becoming quite familiar with their meanings, Laura was presented with a case of metal types containing four sets of the alphabet. She seems to have recognized at once the use of the letters in constructing the words she had learned. Two months afterward she was taught the manual alphabet, and soon became very expert in talking with her fingers.

DEAF MUTE EDUCATION.

"After having learned about a hundred nouns, Laura was instructed in verbs; after another interval, in adjectives and the names of people; not till after a year did she begin learning to write. When she discovered that by means of writing she could communicate her thoughts to others, her joy was boundless, and she eagerly set herself to the task of writing a letter to her mother. After she had been twenty-eight months under instruction, a futile effort was made to teach her abstract qualities, such as "hardness," "softness," etc. This had to be postponed, but her knowledge of various words and their uses was steadily extended.

"Laura was nearly fourteen years old when Charles Dickens visited the asylum and held the interview which he has described in his "American Notes." At that time she had acquired some vague notions about death and a future state. Great care was taken not to force knowledge upon her faster than she could assimilate it. The result has justified the means. Laura Bridgman's education is creditable alike to the method, the instructors, and the pupil.

"Of late years little has been said about her; there must be many friends who will be glad to hear again from this simple-hearted woman, happy under what to most of us would seem the heaviest possible affliction. She is leading a cheerful and pleasant life at the home which she prefers to all the others open to her; the home where her soul first found adequate means of expression: the girls' department of the Massachusetts School for the Blind.

"The domestic affairs of this school are conducted on the cottage system. There are four cottages, built as nearly alike as possible, each of which is presided over by a matron, who has in her family sixteen or seventeen girls and two or more officers. Miss Bridgman belong not exclusively to one family, but rather to the whole department; and moves from cottage to cottage, spending a school year of about eight months in each.

"This year (1886-7) she is living in May Cottage with the senior matron of the department. The house faces the south, and a window filled with bright, thrifty plants is an attraction to the visitor even before he passes the threshold. Nor is he disappointed on entering, for the parlor into which he is ushered has an air of ease and refinement. This is the general sitting-room of the family. Among the ornaments tastefully arranged are some that belong to Miss Bridgman: a comfortable Wakefield chair is her property, and somewhere in the room is a

To Boston March 17th

Dear Sir.
I feel deeply interested in the kindergarten. The sightless children shall be blest with a sunny home by the loving kindness of the Lord. I am happy to do good for the poor children

Laura. D. Bridgman.

FAC-SIMILE OF LETTER WRITTEN BY LAURA BRIDGMAN.

cozy corner, where she keeps her writing material, knitting work and book.

"Passing through a long hall we come to the dining-room, which overlooks the schoolyard. The buildings that we see from the window —very easily, for the nearest one is not more than three rods distant— are the schoolhouses. The one of red brick is the Howe Building, and of the greatest interest, for there Miss Bridgman goes regularly every day to attend one session of the work school. In the upper part of the house are two long corridors, with little bedrooms opening into them. Laura's room is in the southwest corner. It is furnished in black walnut, always exquisitely neat, and well supplied with the various knick-knacks appropriate to a lady's chamber.

"Into this sanctum a few choice friends are sometimes invited for a cozy chat. The care of her little room is one of Laura's daily occupations. She makes the bed and dusts the furniture with scrupulous care. She also dusts the parlors, usually before the rest of the family are up, lifting and replacing ornaments with fingers delicate and sure.

"Invariably an early riser, she is among the last of the older members of the family to go to bed. With apparently few opportunities for usefulness, she is busy every moment of her long day, and time never drags with her.

"She receives and answers many letters; and here perhaps, a few words about her method of writing will not be out of place. A sheet of pasteboard is provided, which has a series of grooves impressed in it. These are each an eighth of an inch wide, and are placed parallel three-eighths of an inch apart. They are to serve as guides for the pencil. The sheet of pasteboard, thus grooved, is put in the folds of a letter-sheet; that is, under the sheet of paper on which the blind person is to write.

"The bodies of the small letters are made in the grooves. Long letters like l and g, and capitals, extend to the plain space above or below. By careful attention to the following directions, one can easily understand how a blind person may be taught to write. Having a mental picture of the writing-board just described, put the point of a pencil at the upper edge of a groove; move it to the left; down to the bottom edge; to the right; up to the top; down, and then to the right again. The result should be a conventionalized a with a square body instead of a round one (▯). With varying directions the entire alphabet, and also the digits, readily appear. But as seeing people seldom

retain in their hand-writing the copper-plate shapes of the copy-book. so the writing of the blind people becomes throughly individual.

"Miss Laura Bridgman's writing, like everything else that she does, is exact and well finished. At times she will sit down and write from memory or something original, but always with a purpose. One Easter morning several of the teachers enjoyed a pleasant surprise which she had prepared for them. She had made a number of copies of her composition known as 'Holy Home,' which is printed in fac-simile of her autograph in Mrs. Mary Swift Lamson's " Life and Education of Laura D. Bridgman." These copies, with slight variations suitable to the season (and the recipient, were enclosed in envelopes directed to the favored ladies, and put at their plates on the breakfast table.

"Very recently Laura presented to the principal of the literary department a paper consisting of numerous well-chosen quotations from the Bible, with a few brief sayings of her own. This was entitled 'Dew-drops for the Kindergarten.' She is averse to writing her autograph for strangers, and frequently asks 'Why do people want my old name?' And yet she is always willing to do it if she can be persuaded that some good cause will thus be served. Probably the number of autographs that she has sold for the benefit of the Kindergarten for the Blind (soon to be opened in one of the suburbs of Boston) may be reckoned by hundreds.

"As said before, Laura Bridgman is never idle. If she goes to call on one of her friends in the institution she never fails to take her worsted work or her exquisite lace. The latter is really extraordinary and shows extreme delicacy of touch; the thread used is very fine, number seventy, sometimes number eighty, and the patterns are graceful and pretty.

"The lace work requires such great care and so much concentration of thought that it is wearisome; poor Laura, who is always ready to earn an honest penny, almost despairs at times of filling her numerous orders. Happily enough to lay her work aside for conversation, she is perfectly willing to sit quietly with a friend and crochet and knit.

"It is often necessary to hold such silent receptions, because the busy officers of the institution cannot put their work away for half hours at a time, as they must in order to talk with Laura. It requires undivided attention to read her rapidly moving fingers, and nearly as much care to form the letters of the manual alphabet in her hand. The alphabet used by Miss Bridgman, by-the-bye, is the single manual alphabet represented among the wood-cuts in the back part of Webster's

DEAF MUTE EDUCATION.

Unabridged Dictionary. Few persons who look hastily at these little cuts think or indeed can know what the manual alphabet has been to Laura and to others cut off from intercourse with their kind by the closing of the senses of sight and hearing. It lay at the foundation of her education even more than the written and printed characters that we esteem so highly. Here is a woman respected and beloved in the little domestic circle that she graces, whose knowledge of passing events is gained solely by the play of the fingers. And most eagerly will she listen with that patient hand, for she loves to learn about people and things. She remarks upon items of news with the artlessness of a child, but with the good sense of an adult.

"Her interest in all domestic and social matters makes her look forward with great pleasure to paying little visits away from the institution. She does not stay away long at a time during the school year, but occasionally goes out for the day, and comes back refreshed and with something pleasant to communicate to the friends at home.

"Laura is not especially fond of books. She reads a little every day, and always has a Bible and a dictionary at hand. The latter she studies assiduously at times, and her quaint use of words new to her is a source of great merriment. Once after she had been looking up the synonyms of 'healthful,' mince-pie was served at dinner; she declined to take any, saying: 'It is not *salubrious*.' For some years she has received a book in raised print as a birth-day gift. After reading it, she usually recommends it to the school-girls and is very willing to lend her copy to anyone of whose carefulness she is assured. During Laura's youth embossed books were a rarity, and perhaps one reason why she is not a greater reader may be that she cannot easily change the habits of her girlhood.

"Tedious as the process is, it gives Laura pleasure to have some one to read to her. With a little skill not difficult to acquire, it is possible to emphasize even when using the manual alphabet, and to make a distinction between prose and poetry by suitable pauses at the end of poetical lines. Laura's mind is so acute that she reads one's meaning however awkwardly expressed. Read in this way, "The Imitation of Christ" is a favorite with her. At one time when she had been much disturbed in mind, having indeed yielded to anger, she was quieted and rested by some little bits from 'The Imitation of Christ,' and expressed her delight in the 'peaceful book,' as she designated it.

"Laura is a child of nature. She loves the sunshine, the fresh air,

the flowers and birds; she is happy to be out-of-doors and to know that the sky is bright, the water blue, the trees bursting into leaf or brilliant with autumnal hues. I have seen her stand by a canary's cage for ten minutes trying to coax the bird to alight on her fingers, and then go away with a saddened, disappointed look, because the bird would not come to her.

"She is fond of little children if they are neat and bright, but she cannot endure the touch of soiled fingers, and she has an instinctive loathing for intellectual weakness whether in child or adult. She is usually correct in her estimates of the intellectual abilities of the people whom she meets, and she forms her opinions on very slight acquaintance.

"Probably few women receive so many and so various callers. People from all quarters of the earth, and of nearly all classes in society come to see her. Sometimes she is bored by visitors, but as a rule, she is courteous and cordial. Never while she has strength to entertain will she desire to withdraw herself from the pleasures of change and society in Boston for her quiet country home in Hanover, New Hampshire.

"To invited guests of the family there is something beautiful in the warmth of Miss Bridgman's hospitality. She considers it her privilege to help to entertain—a privilege granted without the slightest hesitation.

"She has several pretty pieces of china: plates and cups and saucers. These always appear when there is company, and the guest most to be honoured has the most elegant cup and a silver spoon and fork bearing the inscription: 'L. D. B. 1854.'—a precious possession surely, for they are the gift of Charles Summers. After the meal Miss Bridgman, like a careful housewife, herself washes her china and silver, and so she is able to keep it whole and beautiful from year to year.

"There are many days and holidays when the china is used, for Miss Bridgman has a great respect for the custom of observing birthdays and always knows when such occasions come round. Often she makes little presents, and she never forgets to say or do something to make the day happy. But Christmas is the day of all the year! She talks of Santa Claus long before he comes, and shows his benefactions long after he has gone.

"One of her little foibles is a very great admiration for elegancies from foreign lands; lace from France is highly esteemed, a pocket-handkerchief from Dublin is very much admired, imported dresses have a far greater charm than home manufactures. I wonder how many of the ladies in the United States would dare plead 'not guilty' if charged with the same frailty!

"Is it in her case a weakness? Or is it not rather a feeling promoted by human sympathy, a desire to have fellowship with all mankind, to possess, to hold even a thread that makes real to her lives which she has perhaps read of or imagined?

"Laura's sympathies are warm and general. She is happy when unusually pleasant things occur in the home, and will do what she can to make times better. She shares the sadness when affliction comes, and tries in delicate, tender ways to make it easier to bear.

"'Do you think all this rain will quench the 'quakes?' she asked, not long ago, referring to the earthquakes in the South. She had the poor people of Charleston home in her heart, and having probably associated earthquakes with heat and drought, the copious autumn rains recalled the sufferers to her mind, and made her hope that the day of safety had come.

"Another allusion to the Kindergarten for the Blind might need apology were it not at present an all-absorbing interest in Laura's life. So highly does she prize her own education, that the thought of neglected children is most painful to her; and for the last three years her chief delight has been to think about, talk of, and work for the proposed school. Many a time a word from her has been an inspiration for new endeavors.

"We think of her as in utter darkness, in profound silence:

> "A being breathing thoughtful breath,
> A traveller between life and death;
> The reason firm, the temperate will,
> Endurance, foresight, strength and skill; * *
> And yet a spirit still, and bright
> With something of an angel light."

About the time when "American Notes" appeared, a member of the Committee of the Institution reported a case of complete blindness and deafness in a child named Mary Bradley, which had come under his observation at the infant department of the Parochial Schools of the Manchester Union. This excited the curiosity and kind interest of the head master, Mr. Andrew Patterson, and it was proposed he and the member of the committee should examine the case and see if there were any possibility of doing anything with it.

From all that could be ascertained about the child, it appears she was then about seven years old, and that she had lost her sight and hearing about three years previously, having been abandoned by her

DEAF MUTE EDUCATION.

MARY BRADLEY.

mother in a damp cellar while suffering from some virulent disease. The mother, it was understood, was a loose woman, who had left her husband and subsequently her child, and had taken to evil courses. It was believed, at the time the child was received into the Institution for the Deaf and Dumb, that both parents were dead.

Having succeeded in getting the child placed in his charge, Mr. Patterson had next to decide upon some mode of proceeding with her, and the obvious course seemed to be to watch her habits, and to endeavor to adapt his own course and the efforts of those around her to them. With this view she was left for some days to her own resources, in order that the bent of her inclination might be seen and judged of. Finding herself in a new position, she was occupied for a time in becoming acquainted with the locality, and the persons and things by which she was surrounded. She made no attempt to make known her wants by signs, as is usual in the case of the deaf and dumb. If she required help her habit was to shout and scream, and as her utterances were by no means agreeable, every one was interested in relieving her wants. Since her loss of hearing and sight she had been in no position in which signs could be understood, had she made any, but it never seemed to occur to her to do so. In fact, she was at the time one of the most uncouth and wildlooking objects it is well possible to conceive. She had recently had her head shaved in consequence of some disease

DEAF MUTE EDUCATION.

in the skin of the scalp, and with a crouching, groping attitude, she had more the appearance of a scared and timid animal seeking some mode of escape from danger or unpleasant position, than of a human being endowed with a rational soul.

The first step in teaching seemed to be to make her acquainted with the names of the object around her. With this view, then, Mr. Patterson selected those objects which differed materially in form from each other, viz., a *pen*, a *book* and a *slate*. As the visible letters could not be submitted to her, the signs used by the deaf and dumb were given on the fingers instead, Mr. Patterson giving the signs by touching her fingers with his, in the proper form. Thus the *pen* was placed in her hands; she felt its firm, elastic quality, etc.; then the letters *pen* were signed on her fingers, and an endeavour made to indicate to her that the signs meant the object which she had been handling. The other words *book* and *slate* were indicated in the same way; but she failed to understand the connection between these arbitrary signs and the things handled. It never seemed to occur to her that the signs had any reference to the objects.

In the case of children who can hear or see, the sounds of the letters or the forms of the signs are at once a key to their application to the object named, but in this case there was no clue to the meaning, as at present they had neither sound nor form to her mind. An hour or two, day after day, was devoted to the accomplishment of this first and all-important step; but the labour seemed entirely without effect. No progress towards success was made, and every day the work had to be commenced anew, and unfortunately was followed by the same results as on the previous days, without any progress. Every means were tried to arrive at some degree of success. The appliances were varied as much as possible, but still apparently without any intelligence on the part of the pupil. Her kind and assiduous teacher could only devote to her the hours in which he could be spared from the routine work of a large school. He continued these attempts for four or five weeks, and almost in despair of any good results began to think of abandoning his efforts, at least for a period; when all at once, like a sudden burst of sunshine, her countenance brightened up one day with a full intelligence beaming in it. She had found the key to the mystery! Placing her hand on each of the objects separately, she gave the name of each on her fingers, or rather signed them on the fingers of her teacher as her mode of describing them.

DEAF MUTE EDUCATION.

Thus the first step was attained at last, and the chief difficulty cleared away for overcoming the next. It was a comparatively easy matter now to proceed and enlarge the vocabulary of the names of the objects most familiar to her. Mr. Patterson then cut out the letters of the alphabet in cardboard, and gummed them to a sheet of stiff pasteboard, so that they stood in relief, and could be sharply felt and distinguished from each other by the fingers. By this means she soon became acquainted with all their forms, and mentally associated—say *pen*—with the signs upon her fingers and the object which these signs represented. Her progress now became daily more and more evident. She took great delight in her work, and with the limited time at Mr. Patterson's disposal, it was difficult to keep pace with her desire for the knowledge of names. From these she was taught the quality of things. When new words of this kind were intended to be taught, the objects were generally placed before her, as an illustration of comparison; for instance—a large book and a small one, a light object and a heavy one, thick and thin, rough and smooth, hard and soft, sweet and sour. Objects possessing opposite qualities were placed within her reach, and she very readily acquired the words to express them. Thus the work went on step by step, every day's lesson being a preparatory one for the next day. Verbs were taught much in the same way, the word being given with the action: standing, sitting, walking; eating, drinking, laughing, crying, etc., generally in the form of the present participle, and in connection with a noun, as being an easy change from the adjectives—as, a boy standing, a girl crying, etc.

At length the great inconvenience presented itself of the want of a lesson-book adapted to meet the case. In order to supply this want, a case of type for printing in relief was obtained, and some lessons were printed, which were readily deciphered by the pupil through the sense of touch. It was, however, soon discovered that the operation of composing the type was an exercise which was not only very amusing to her, but also very instructive. A little box was constructed in which she could arrange the type in sentences, etc., which were dictated to her by natural signs, the teacher using her hands in the same way as he would use his own to sign similar sentences to a seeing deaf child, and this became a never-failing source of interest. It made her familiar with the various modes of construction,—the greatest difficulty which the deaf and dumb have to encounter. Every new word was at once applied to its appropriate meaning.

DEAF MUTE EDUCATION.

The effect of the dawning of this new world of intellectual life upon the temper and disposition of Mary Bradley was, at this point of her education, very unmistakable. She had hitherto been of a fretful, impatient, and very irritable temper, crying and screaming without any apparent cause; but as she made progress in her studies, this irritability gradually softened down, and she became daily more and more subdued in disposition and manner. Still at intervals, more or less prolonged, she would have fits of fretfulness and passions, which would end in a few hours in tears, when she would again resume her quiet and placid manner. These occasional bursts would appear to have been a necessity with her. They seemed like an accumulation of humours which would burst out and expend themselves, and this give relief for a time. Mr. Patterson and the kind friends around her soon discovered that during these paroxysms, the best and simplest course was to leave her to herself.

The time occupied in teaching her to write was enormous as compared with that expended on children possessing their proper faculties. It was a work of incessant and interminable repetition; but Mr. Patterson had resolved that it must be done, and it was done accordingly.

Having once learned to write, she was enabled to correspond with friends at a distance, and to interchange letters with her sisters in deprivation across the Atlantic, Laura Bridgman, who was kind enough to send her a tablet, such as she herself used. Now it must be distinctly understood that the results thus happily arrived at were attained under circumstances very different to those in which the education of Laura Bridgman was carried on—not to mention the great difference between the condition of Mary Bradley when she was rescued from the degrading and cruel associations of a pauper school, and the domestic surroundings in which Laura Bridgman had been brought up in a bright and loving home, under the care of a tender mother. From this home she was transferred to the charge of Dr. Howe, and by him placed under the special care of the lady teacher whose sole duty and pleasure it was to see to her every want, and act as her instructress. Mary Bradley, on the contrary, could only receive continuous attention for any length of time from Mr. Patterson when the duties of a large establishment permitted: and then he could only devote, what would otherwise have been his leisure, to her instruction.

At the period when Mary Bradley had been under instruction some four or five years an application was made to the Institution for the admission of a little boy suffering under the same sad privation.

DEAF MUTE EDUCATION.

THE TWO BLIND DEAF-MUTES.

Joseph Hague was the son of a deaf and dumb mother who had been educated in the Institution. He was born deaf, and became blind before he was two years old. At the period of his reception in the School for the Deaf and Dumb he was eight years old, and at once became the fellow-pupil of Mary Bradley.

On his admission he was allowed a few days to make himself familiar with the new position in which he was placed. It was very amusing to watch his explorations and to see the ready intelligence with which he made his observation.

Joseph Hague showed a considerable amount of determination and combativeness when he met with opposition. On one occasion he was walking up the school-room, in there are two or three iron pillars to to support the floor above, and forgetting that such was the case he struck his forehead against one of them and recoiled from it. He rubbed his forehead for an instant, and then walked deliberately up to the pillar and kicked it violently.

This boy, being born deaf and dumb and having been under the care of his mother, herself a deaf-mute, was thoroughly acquainted with the signs used by the deaf children of her age, and consequently the first steps in the course of his instruction were easily overcome. The pro-

gress made by the two far outstripped any anticipations which could be formed on the subject from what had been previously effected by Mr. Patterson's attention to Mary Bradley only. The knowledge of things gradually led on to those of a more abstract character, and enabled their kind teacher to show the relation between cause and effect and by means of things of a lower nature to reach the higher. A knowledge of Scripture History and of God's care for His chosen people was imparted.

During the progress of these children in their instruction, many points peculiar to themselves and to their condition could not fail to manifest themselves. One pecularity, which is perhaps more striking than any other, was the appearance of a perception which seemed like a new sense. The quickness of apprehension and understanding of what was passing around them seemed so complete and so accurate, that it was impossible to conceive how the mind grasped the information unless such was the case. The boy was of rather a mischievous disposition, and was fond of amusing himself by teasing and annoying his companion; but it is a rather singular fact that the moment Mr. Patterson entered the room he became conscious of the fact, and instantly ceased his amusement. No doubt he had become accustomed to the vibration caused by the opening and shutting of the door, and by the step of his teacher, for he could distinguish the latter from that of every one else; and would frequently stop Mr. Patterson in the room to ask a question. In addition to this, however, both these children would receive impressions when the sense of feeling could not be acted upon, and they would be aware of facts which could not reach the mind by any of the known senses. For instance, they would sit together and hold long conversations upon each other's fingers, and while doing so Mr. Patterson would approach them with the greatest caution, and in a manner which could produce no vibration, either from his step or the movement of his body, yet they became immediately conscious of his presence, ceased their conversation, and one would inform the other that Mr. Patterson was behind them. This occured over and over again in order to test their intelligence; every precaution and means being taken to approach without their knowledge, but always with the same results. It was quite impossible to discover by what mode they discovered the fact of the presence of their instructors; all that could be ascertained was that they did discover it at once.

As a further illustration of mental peculiarity it may be stated that

DEAF MUTE EDUCATION.

they had an instinctive perception of character. When strangers approached them they at once put out their hands to touch them, and having done so, would either feel attracted to them or repulsed by them. In the former case they would soon put themselves on the most familiar terms with them; in the latter they would hold themselves aloof. It was the same among their school-fellows. With some, the boy especially, was on the most familiar terms, and could take any liberty with them, making them the slaves of his will; while with others he held little or no intercourse, and never voluntarily associated with them.

The sense of touch in these two children was exceedingly acute. Every person in the Institution for the Deaf and Dumb was known and recognised by them by the touch, and though many schemes were adopted occasionally to puzzle them, yet they always discovered it and named the right person. On one occasion the late Bishop of Manchester, Dr. Prince Lee, having brought some friend, to visit the Institution, wished to test the boy's ability to find any one of his companions who might be named. He did so without a single failure, though they were all mixed together, and not in their usual places in the school. The boys were then made to exchange clothes, and one of them presented himself to be named. Hague at once named the boy who belonged to the clothes. On being told that he was wrong, he proceeded to manipulate the hands and features, and without hesitation gave the right name. After failing in the first instance his suspicions were awakened and he could not be deceived a second time.

One would imagine that persons so shut out from the influences that are apt to excite and stimulate vanity in dress, would be quite free from any weakness of this kind; but it is not so. Mary Bradley was quite a connoisseur in dress, and was fond of feeling the dresses and trimmings of those within her reach, and giving her opinion. On one occasion two ladies, dressed in every respect alike, both as to pattern and material, came under her manipulation. She said, or rather signed, that they were very nice, but that one dress was much better than the other. The ladies said she was mistaken, as they were exactly alike, being made of the same material, cut from the same piece of fabric. She, however, insisted that they were not alike, and that one dress was much better than the other. No difference could be detected by any one else; but Mary Bradley was found to be right. From subsequent inquiry it was discovered that the person from whom the material was bought had not sufficient of the one piece, supplied by the same manufacturer,

from which he cut sufficient for one of the dresses, believing it to be in every respect the exact quality of the other. From the delicacy of the touch of this deaf, dumb, and blind girl, the fact was detected that one piece was of superior quality to the other.

Having acquired a tolerable facility in basket-making, and becoming impatient under the restraints of the Institution, Hague became desirous of leaving. Both his parents were living, and could understand him and converse with him: it was therefore thought advisable that he should quit the school and the surveillance of his worthy and kind teacher, Mr. Patterson, who had providently been enabled to do so much for him; and be placed under the supervision of his father and mother.

Mary Bradley, without a relative known to any one connected with the Institution, remained in it and regarded it as her permanent home. Indeed, she was generally considered as an indispensable part of it! Her conscious life had been, as it were, awakened within its walls and developed in its school-room. She scarcely knew of any world beyond—at least, not in this life. During the last seven or eight years of her earthly existence she suffered much from abscesses, which formed in various parts of her body. She gradually wasted away and died June, 1866, in her 26th year, firmly believing in a future life of happiness through Christ, leaving her bodily privations and afflictions behind her. Nothing can be clearer than the facts that the problem of the education of the deaf, dumb and blind was as fully solved in her case as in those of the more widely and popularly known instances of Laura Bridgman and Oliver Caswell, at the Massachusetts Institution.

Joseph Hague died in the Sheffield Workhouse on the 28th February, 1879. His parents had removed there on his leaving school at Manchester. At that time the writer was employed at Sheffield to organize the Association for Adult Deaf-mutes, having for its object their religious and secular instruction. Joseph Hague attended these services regularly and took great delight in them. This continued until 1869, when circumstances arose which became necessary to remove him to the workhouse, where he was placed under the special care of an assistant. He was a good basketmaker, and partly supported himself after leaving school. He continued to work at that trade while in the Union, where special privileges were allowed him by the guardians. His greatest pleasure was to be allowed to attend the Sabbath services, his deaf-mute friends taking a delight in conveying instruction to him upon his fingers, and in other ways administering to his wants, including

DEAF MUTE EDUCATION.

taking him to their homes; and even the poorest ungrudgingly shared their frugal meal with him. A great portion of his time whilst in the Workhouse was occupied in reading and committing to memory portions of Scripture, and repeating upon his fingers the portions so learnt, and in this manner he had acquired a store of Scripture knowledge that would put to shame many of his more favoured fellow-creatures. On these occasions he would have a number of words committed to memory of which he did not know the meaning, and would most anxiously seek an explanation of them. It was also his delight to read the biography of great and good men, which books he obtained from the lending library for the blind; and it is a most remarkable fact he rarely forgot any portion of such works, and was very conscientious in all his dealings.

JOSEPH HAGUE.
Departed this Life on the 28th February, 1879.

Wall'd in by Deafness, Dumbness, Blindness, all!
Could Life exist beneath that dreadful pall?
It did. Life, Love were there: The living Soul
Beat hot against the bars that held it in,
Striving among the best, to reach the goal,
And, through CHRIST's Death, immortal Life to **win**.

With such a chain he laboured, on his way:
From such a chain the Soul has burst away:
The heart which throbb'd with love, hope and fear;
The Mind which strove within that dungeon drear:
The Eyes which longed in vain for earthly light,
See face to face, in GOD's most holy sight,
Kind Death hath bid the captive soul go free,
Where the Deaf hear, Dumb sing, and Sightless see.

D. B.

It is very fortunate that the number of blind deaf-mutes in the world is very small. There are nearly a million blind people in the world and over 800,000 deaf-mutes, but the number of blind deaf-mutes probably does not exceed 50. Of the few who are on record, the following may be mentioned:

1. James Mitchell, born 1795, near Inverness, Scotland. Uneducated.
2. Hannah **Lamb**, London, 1808, accidentally burned to death. Uneducated.
3. Laura **Bridgman, born** at Hanover, N. H., 21st December, 1829. Educated by **Dr. Howe,** still living (1879.)
4. Oliver **Caswell,** South Boston. Educated at same place as Bridgman. 1841.
5. Lucy Reed, **South Boston, only party educated.**

DEAF MUTE EDUCATION.

6. Mary Bradley, born at Manchester **and** educated there, 1845. **Was a** correspondent of Laura Bridgman.

7. Joseph Hague, the school-mate of Mary Bradley, also born at Manchester. Died 28th February, 1879 at Sheffield.

8. Catherine St. Just Taskey, born in 1848 in Lower Canada, partly educated at the Protestant Institution for Deaf-mutes at Montreal in 1871.

9. James **H. Coton, pupil in the New York** Institution for Deaf-mutes, 1878.

Sweden **is** reported to have 20 blind deaf-mutes, an enormous number for **any** country in Europe. In the New York Institution there is a curious **case of a** boy deaf and dumb and without **arms**, who is being successfully instructed by Dr. Peet, who has taught **him to** write with **a long pencil attached** to the stumps of his **arms**

CHAPTER IX.

AN EASY METHOD OF TEACHING DEAF-MUTES AT HOME.

For the benefit of those who desire to do all they can to instruct their own children before sending them to an institution, the following description has been prepared of the method to be pursued. It is hoped that all having mute children will spare no pains in their home instruction, and however little progress **may** be secured, it will still be of value to the **child.** In some cases it may **be** weeks **or** months before the child **is able to** write a single word, but **if the** plan here explained is perseveringly **carried** out, success is certain.

The method here presented is not **a new one** : it has been in vague more than half **a century,** and is still **used** with great success by some of the best instructors **of deaf-mutes.**

In addition **to writing** words and sentences, let the child **also** spell them by means of the **manual** alphabet, of which engravings **are** given in this book.

In memorizing the alphabets, the best way is to learn throughly each horizontal row of characters before commencing **the** next one below. If this is done, the alphabet **will** be perfectly mastered in less than an **hour.** Use either the one or the two handed alphabets as you like best.

It is also well to **use** every means to preserve the vocal utterance of the child, for though hearing cannot be recovered, speech may, in many **cases,** be retained, if the child **is** constantly practised in the use of its voice.

The child may be taught as early as the age of three or four to write a few words. From that age, until six or seven, he should be practised by the method here given, and then **sent** to some institution, where his progress will be very rapid if this preparatory home training has been well performed.

HOW TO BEGIN—FIRST STEP.

Begin by writing in a plain round hand the name of some common object. Show to the child first the object and then the name, pointing from one to the other until he sees that the name stands for the object. Get him to copy **the** word, and when he has mastered it, teach him **another** in the same way. Always write *the* before the names of objects.

As above explained teach the following list of words containing all the letters of the alphabet:

the book,	the cup,	the mug,	the jar,
the key,	the quill,	the feather,	the box,
the pen,	the watch,	the glove,	the zinc.

Besides these, the names father, mother, the child's own name, and those of his brothers and sisters, should be taught.

SENTENCES.

As soon as the child can write the names of five or six objects, sentences may be taught. To do this a short direction to do something, as, *touch the box*, is shown to the pupil. Then the teacher himself touches the box and gets the child to imitate him. After several repetitions the child is made to copy the sentences, *I touched the box*, as the proper way of expressing what he has done. He is then directed in writing to touch some other object of which he knows the name, and, if he does not understand, the teacher again explains as before. This is repeated frequently until the pupil, on being shown a direction to touch a familiar object, will at once go and do so. This process of writing a short direction, showing the child what it means by simply performing the action indicated, and then having him copy the proper form of sentence to express what he has done, is to be always carried out. Proceed in the same manner with many examples like the following:

Touch the key.	Touch the table.
Touch the cup.	Touch the chair.
Touch the mug.	Touch father.
Touch the jar.	Touch mother.
Touch the zinc.	Touch John.
Touch the watch.	Touch Mary.

The teacher must touch objects himself, and get the child to describe what he has done, by using *you* in place of *I*, thus:

You touched the key.	You touched the fork.
You touched the shovel.	You touched the glove.

A third person should also be asked to do something in the presence of the child, and the latter taught to describe it as:

Father touched the slate.	John touched the fan.
Mother touched the pail.	Mary touched the jug.
John touched Mary.	Mary touched John.

When the pupil has became expert in these exercises, directed him to touch two or more objects, which must at first be placed together before him. Vary all of the foregoing exercises, as in the examples given below:

DEAF MUTE EDUCATION.

I touched the hat and the key.
I touched the chair and the table.
You touched the book and the shovel.
You touched the pencil and the slate.
Father touched the door and the hat.
John touched the knife and the fork.

The same exercises should now be continued, with the following words in place of *touch*. Each word **must be** used quite often and thoroughly mastered before a new **one is** given:

bring,	open,	shut,	kick,	strike,	throw,
hit,	push,	pull,	gather,	break,	pare,
tear,	cut,	lift,	bite,	wash,	wipe,
sweep,	eat,	drink,	smell,	taste,	slap,
clean,	whip,	raise,	pat,	rub,	drop,
bind,	shake,	roll,	pinch,	lock,	unlock,
cover,	uncover,	toss,	fill,	empty,	**scrape,**
faced,	light,	punch,	**tickle,**	comb,	**scratch,**

PHRASES.

The following phrases, it will be seen, are as easily explained as any of the single words above given, by merely performing the **act** indicated. These should be used very often, and with as **many** objects as are appropriate to them:

sit on, stand on, kneel on, write on, play on, run on, jump on, **roll** on, stand in, stand under, walk to, go into, walk into, run into, go out of, run out of, put on, take off, jump over, stand before, stand behind, stand beside, stand near, walk around, walk across, stand between, point to, bow to, shake hands.

The following examples will show **how** the above phrases are to be used:

I sat on the chair.
I stood on the box.
I went to the table.
You ran on the grass.
You turned off the gas.
You walked around the chair.
John walked across the room.
John stood before father.
Mr. Smith put on his coat.

I stood in the tub.
I blew out the match.
I walked to the gate.
You went into the house.
You jumped over the stool.
You sat near the fire.
Mary ran from the dog.
Mary stood behind mother.
The cat jumped from the chair.

I stood between the chair and the table.
I stood between the door and the window.
John sat between father and mother.
Father stood between John and Mary.
You walked from the chair to the table.
You ran from the door to the gate.

COLOR, SIZE, FORM, ETC.

The process of teaching color, size, form, possession and numbers **will** now be considered. In explaining these, some object having the qualities described by the words used must always be placed before the

child; otherwise the meaning **cannot be** made clear to him. **He must** always learn by seeing, handling, smelling and tasting the objects.

To explain color, make a number of balls of yarn of different colors. These should be of black, white, brown, gray, purple, red, orange, yellow, green, blue, violet. **Pieces** of ribbon, cloth or sticks painted of these colors, will **answer as** well. At the printer's, cards of most of th above colors can be had for a trifling sum.

Place one of the **balls,** say black, before the child, and write the direction—*Touch the black ball,* and proceed as before explained. Continue this with all **the** colors in turn.

Also, **explain** the following **words** of opposite meaning, with suitable **objects.** The contrast in meaning is a great **help towards understanding them: and for this** reason first one and then the other should be used:

<blockquote>hot, cold; hard, soft; wet, dry; clean, dirty; sweet, sour; thick, thin; fat, lean; sharp, dull; new, old; high, low; full, empty; smooth, rough; straight, crooked; wide, narrow; sound, rotten; fragrant, fetid; light, heavy; etc.</blockquote>

Size will now be considered. **Get two** objects of the same kind, but differing much in size, as stones, potatoes, apples, books, etc., and with these teach the meaning of the words *large* and *small.* Place both before the pupil and direct him to touch one, and give him **the proper form of** sentence to describe what he has been doing. **Do the same with the** other, and **repeat until the** words are understood.

ARITHMETIC.—NUMBERS.

In teaching numbers, get stones, sticks, beans, or marbles, to count with. Then give the following directions, and **show the child how to** carry them out and express what he had done:

<blockquote>Put one bean on the table.
Put two beans on the table.
Put three beans on the table.</blockquote>

This exercise may **be continued** until all **the** numbers up to one hundred have been learned. Let the child learn both the names and the characters **used to** represent the numbers. Let the teacher himself, as well as other persons, put objects in different places, and teach the child to describe what they do. In this exercise, language as well as numbers are being learned at the same time, as the examples here given will show:

<blockquote>I put four books on the table.
I put nine stones in the pail.
I put fifteen beans under the table.
You put one stone and seven sticks in the hat.</blockquote>

DEAF MUTE EDUCATION.

ADDITION.

To teach addition, put down two beans before the child, and pointing from one to the other, give him the sentence, One and one are two, to copy. When this is mastered place one bean at his left hand and two at his right, and let him write, One and two are three. Then, with one and three beans, placed in the same way, teach him to write, One and three are four. Go on in this way up to One and ten are eleven. Keep on until the child can write out this part of the table correctly.

SUBTRACTION.

When we come to subtraction we have simply to place a row of beans before the child, and taking away one or more, give him the proper form in which to express the operation.

Begin by placing two beans before him, and then taking away one, write One from two leaves one. So proceed up to One from eleven leaves ten. When this is mastered, change the places of the sentences and let the child fill up the blank spaces thus :

    One from six leaves———.
    One from two leaves———.
    One from nine leaves———.

Proceed in this manner until the tables in subtraction are thoroughly mastered.

MULTIPLICATION.

In multiplication the beans are to be arranged in groups containing an equal number. First place one bean before the child, and another a little way from it, and have him write, Two times one are two. Then place two beans in each group, and write two times two are four. Next put three beans in each group, and write Two times three are six. In this way proceed to Two times ten are twenty. As before, finish by changing the places of the sentences and leaving a blank for the pupil to fill up. Teach the remaining tables in the same way.

DIVISION.

In division there may be a little more difficulty, but patience will overcome all. Here the process consists in arranging a row of beans before the child, and then separating it into groups containing the same number.

Place two beans before the pupil. With both hands separate them and draw each a little to one side. Then write, One is in two twice. Now separate in the same way a row of four beans, and write Two is in

four twice. In this manner continue till Ten is in twenty twice, has been reached. Change the places of the sentences, and proceed as before described. Finish all the tables in division in this way.

The teaching of fractions is far less difficult than may at first sight appear.

Let there be some apples in the room, and give the child the direction, Bring me one apple. Take the apple, and in his sight divide it into two equal parts. Then write the direction, Bring me one-half of the apple, explaining the phrase one-half of the apple, by pointing to it and then to the object. Then write, Bring me two halves of the apple. As in the previous exercises, let the child be practised frequently, until he has mastered this. Show him that one-half and $\frac{1}{2}$ means the same thing.

PART II.

HISTORY OF DEAF-MUTE EDUCATION

IN CANADA.

THE RISE AND PROGRESS OF DEAF-MUTE EDUCATION IN CANADA.

By JOHN BARRETT McGANN, *with continuation by* MRS. E. TERRILL, *née* E. McGANN.

J. B. McGANN.

"JOHN BARRETT McGANN was born in the City of Kilkenny, Ireland, on the 25th of December, 1810. He was educated principally in the Village of Cloumellon, County of Westmeath, whither his parents removed when he was quite young. After leaving school he served the usual term as Land Surveyor in Castledowndelvin, and afterwards joined the Ordnance Survey of Ireland, under Gen. Renwick, who now resides in London, Ont. He was first married in 1829 to Cecelia Webb, at the residence of John P. Curran, the eminent Irish

DEAF MUTE EDUCATION.

lawyer, who was a cousin to Miss Webb. After his marriage Mr. McGann taught school for fourteen years—ten years in the city of Dublin. His wife died in 1850, and in 1852 he married Maria Gale, a cousin to W. E. Shanley, the well-known contractor. This second wife died in 1854, and in December of the same year he left Ireland for America. Arriving in New York, he sought the service of an old friend—Dr. Prime, then connected with the New York Observer. While in the Doctor's service he met and was introduced to the President of the New York Institution for the Deaf and Dumb. By this means he became interested in the education of the unfortunate class, with whose interests he afterwards became so closely identified.

"In 1855 Mr. McGann came to Canada, which was his destination when leaving Ireland. He landed in Toronto, bearing letters of introduction to Dr. Hodgins, Deputy Minister of Education, and other prominent educationalists. Shortly after his arrival he was appointed to a position in the Toronto Grammar School with Dr. Howe, which he filled for some time. He was also employed as private tutor in the families of Col. Gzowski and Hon. D. L. Macpherson and others. During this time, however, his interest in the education of deaf-mutes, first awakened in New York, did not slumber. He made enquiries, collected a few pupils, and opened the first deaf and dumb school for this Province in Toronto in 1858." About three months afterwards he gave the first public examination of his school, which elicited much interest, and was the beginning of a work which we now see so admirably developed in the Provincial Institution for the Education of the Deaf and Dumb. At this examination Mr. McGann proposed that a society be formed in the city of Toronto to assist him in the organization of a deaf and dumb school. His proposition was acted upon, and the school continued to be conducted by this society until the spring of 1864, when it was closed for want of pupils. Mr. McGann had, however, withdrawn from the school some time previously, and had opened one of his own. To this latter the beneficiaries of the various County Councils and the Government grant were appropriated, and it soon became strong in the number of pupils and public patronage.

"Mr. McGann encountered many difficulties in the work which he had undertaken, but with a zeal that admitted no discouragement he labored on, and gradually extended the sphere of his usefulness and benevolence. In 1864, owing to inducements held out by influential parties, he removed his school to Hamilton. With improved facilities and a more generous support, he gathered about him an able staff of

DEAF MUTE EDUCATION.

assistants, and began to attract public attention from the remote parts of the Province. The Hamilton School gradually developed into an Institution, and was located in Dundurn Castle, the residence of the late Sir Allan McNab, situated on the "Mountain," and overlooking the city and bay. Here Mr. McGann continued to labor with his assistants until the opening of the Provincial Deaf and Dumb Institute at Belleville in 1870, when he was appointed one of the principal teachers. About a year before his death his health began to fail, and he was obliged to resign his charge sometime in 1879.

"Prof. McGann has been called the pioneer of deaf-mute education in Ontario, and this brief memoir will show that he was well entitled to the distinction. With limited means and in the face of a prejudiced opposition he founded the first school for the instruction of this class, and made its influence felt throughout the country. In addition to all he has accomplished as a teacher, he wrote volumes in support of the work so dear to his heart, and travelled extensively to collect means and information. He was the author of several valuable books, treating on deaf mutes and their education. Two of these—" Home Education for the Deaf and Dumb," and " Suffering Humanity,"—have been read by many, and have accomplished much good.

"Mr. McGann was a ready writer, and had a wide range of general information. He was social and warm hearted, delighting in the society of his friends. Up to the very hour of his dissolution he maintained a warm interest in the welfare of the mutes, and frequently inquired about the progress of the work at the Institute. In the death of John B. McGann the deaf and dumb of Canada lost a warm friend and benefactor."

[The following commencing account was the last production of the lamented author.]

Walking along Spadina Avenue, in the City of Toronto, on a fine evening, in May, 1858, I met a very nice girl about 15 years of age. She was running from a boy who had a brick in his hand. The boy followed the girl to strike her with the brick. He was very angry because the girl annoyed him very much. I stopped him and took the brick from him. The boy was deaf and dumb, and his left arm paralyzed. Three weeks after this happened I met two other deaf-mutes, and this led me to search about and find more. My inquiries ended when I found that there were 30 deaf and dumb in the city of Toronto.

Alderman Baxter was at this time School Trustee and bore a high character for kindness. I asked him for a spare room in the Phœbe Street School. He gave it to me with pleasure.

DEAF MUTE EDUCATION.

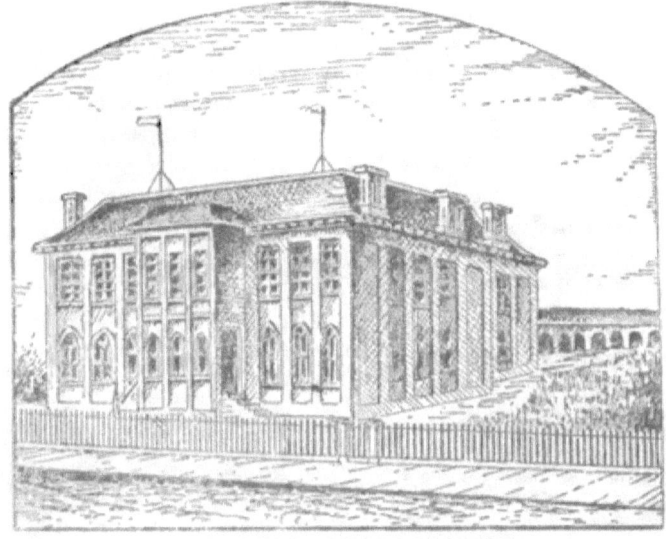

PHOEBE STREET SCHOOL.

On the 22nd day of June, 1858, I opened a school with four very interesting pupils. I taught them for three months, and they made good progress in language for the time under instruction. Having got the use of St. Lawrence Hall free of expense I got up large placards, stating that an examination of deaf-mutes would be given on the 3rd of September to show what could be done to lighten the affliction of the deaf and dumb. The hall was filled with the *elite* of the city. The Rev. Dr. McCaul was chairman, and Mr. Moss, now Chief Justice, was the speaker. The examination was very successful in its object by exciting pity for the deaf and dumb.

The late Rev. Thomas S. Kennedy stood up at the close of the meeting and proposed that "A school be opened to admit all the deaf-mutes of the city, and that a meeting be held next day to appoint a committee to carry the resolution into effect."

Another examination was held on the 9th of December, at which Bishop Strachan, the Hon. George Brown, many gentleman and clergymen sat on the platform. The St. Lawrence Hall was full of people. A committee was appointed to manage the Institution and provide money for it. The committee consisted of fourteen members of the Church of England, and eight of other churches. The first act of the committee

was to apply to the County Council for assistance. They gave a grant of $400, next they applied to the Government and received $1,000.

The late Dr. H. Peet, of the New York Institution, wrote a letter to the committee, stating that I did not understand the deaf and dumb, nor did the deaf and dumb understand me, as I did not use the sign language. He also sent his son, with his beautiful and accomplished wife, to Toronto to give a lecture on this elegant and graceful language as a means of instruction. An accident happened on the railway, and he was obliged to return to New York and never reached Toronto.

I firmly believe Dr. Peet has changed his opinions as to the merits of the signs, as he is one of the most able advocates of the present day for object teaching, and has published a most valuable text book, illustrating the true system.

The letter to which I referred in my last was used against me by a certain Rev. gentleman of the committee, and I was informed by the late Joseph Hartman, M.P., (the Warden of the York County Council then in session), that the grant of $400 would be stopped. I was determined then to disprove all the false allegations made against me. Before the whole Council I asked permission to give an examination of my deaf-mute children in presence of that body, which was readily granted.

The Council were both astonished and pleased at the progress of the fourteen deaf-mutes examined before them. I used Peet's Elementary Lessons, and in nine months my pupils had reached the 110th lesson. During an examination which lasted an hour the pupils made not a single error. The Council then drew up a resolution recommending my school to the patronage of all the County Councils in Upper Canada. A few days after, the Rev. gentleman (before mentioned) at a Sunday School festival gave three cheers for Mr. McGann, and a year afterward on his return from a visit to England the committee gave the following in their report: "The late visit of their secretary, the Rev. T. T. Kennedy, to England has enabled them to compare this progress with that of the pupils of institutions long established in the United Kingdom, and the result of that comparison is highly favorable to the system of instruction adopted in this school." Thus thanks to a kind Providence I surmounted these great difficulties, and made two of my enemies my best friends.

But another cloud as portentious loomed black in the horizon. Archbishop Lynch, at my request, visited my school. He was well pleased with his visit, and on leaving presented each pupil with a sum of money; asked for a half holiday, and hired an omnibus to take them

OLD GRAMMAR SCHOOL, JARVIS STREET.

all for a drive to the Lunatic Asylum, where Dr. Workman gave us a grand lunch and showed us through the building,

A funny little incident occurred here, Charles Howe was a sweet and interesting little fellow of four or five years old. One of the women thought that Dr. Workman was about to shut him up. She ran to the open fire place, quickly slipped her hand in behind the fender, seized a live coal and ran after the Dr. to apply it to him. He nimbly got out of her way, whereupon the nurse put her where she could not injure any one, and wound up the burned hand.

A short time after upon another visit of the Archbishop I proposed that the Roman Catholic children of the country be brought into the school, and that a Roman Catholic teacher be appointed. His Lordship immediately took up my views and offered to pay the salary himself if I trained the teacher. But, alas! this last act of mine made the committee think I needed watching, so they concluded to appoint a superintendent over me to swallow up the funds which ought to have gone for the education of these poor children who knew not God. However the Archbishop very liberally gave a donation of seventy dollars to assist me.

I entertained a heartfelt gratitude to Dr. and Mrs. Howe for their many acts of kindness to myself and pupils during the time we occupied the room in the old grammar school buildings. These kind friends never had occasion to make a complaint against any of the pupils during these twelve months. On the fourth of October, 1856, my daughter Effie, now Mrs. Terrill, commenced her duties as assistant teacher without salary. In fact all the money I had received for eighteen months was $680, *vide* Report for 1860.

In the later part of 1859 I received a valuable present of "Elementary Text Book" from the late learned President of the New York Institution, H. P. Peet, L.L.D., and one of his principal teachers, Prof. Morris, sent many encouraging letters.

At this time there were nineteen pupils in attendance, amongst these I might mention many who have led useful and industrious lives, which maketh my heart to rejoice. If I might particularize any I would mention Minnie Rumley, the late Mrs. McCoy; Susan Speers, now Mrs. Hambly; Isabella Hambly (Mrs. A. Leeson), Charles J. Howe, John and Henry Moore, and Norman V. Lewis. Children then, now grown to man's and woman's estate, and by their irreproachable conduct would be a credit to any institution in the world.

QUEEN STREET SCHOOL, TORONTO.

In May, 1860, we removed to No. 490 Queen street west, to commodious buildings, with a large garden, which had formerly been occupied as a boarding school for boys. The house, as well as the general management, was placed under the superintendence of Dr. Morris. while I took the educational department.

DEAF MUTE EDUCATION.

This year we inaugurated the system of holding meetings throughout the country to excite an interest on behalf of the deaf and dumb, as well as to raise funds for the Institution. The first Government grant was also made of $1,000. The County Council grants amounted to $829. The whole amount of monies received this year was $3,336.85.

The following, I copy from the Report of 1860, showing the state of my department:

"The progress made by the pupils generally is highly satisfactory, and reflects great credit on the Master and assistant teachers. I may here briefly allude to the method of instruction adopted by Mr. McGann, and used by him for the last year. Although the plan is not new absolutely, it certainly is so in its application to the deaf and dumb *palmam qui meruit ferat*. By it the use of the sign language is done away with; all instruction is communicated to the pupil by writing or spelling the word in full or showing him the object; he thus is saved the necessity of translating from the arbitrary sign into the English language before he can come at the idea of the word. I have no doubt that in this there is a saving to the pupil of at least one-third; while his ideas on all subjects becomes much more definite and precise."

Also the following from my own Report to the Committee:

"Their vocabulary embraces the plural of nouns, two tenses of verbs associated directly with visible actions, and the incorporation of adjectives of color and dimension into phrases, and simple sentences taken from objects and actions presented to the eye, ignoring *intoto* the natural and conventional sign language in the process of instruction, the object in view, being to associate the idea of the pupil directly with the object or action, and thereby enable him, the more easily to arrive at the idea of printed or written words, by the use of alphabetic language as the intermediary between the idea and the word. This is in order to train the mind of the deaf and dumb pupil to think in that language, which must, of necessity, become the vehicle of expressing his thoughts; in other words to make the English language his vernacular."

I am deeply impressed with the firm conviction that the deaf and dumb pupil, who translates from signs, can only write composition after the same manner, in which a college student writes a Latin or Greek composition, if he first writes his thoughts in English, and afterward translates them into Latin or Greek, I aim to train my pupils to think in the English language.

DEAF MUTE EDUCATION.

It is a new feature in deaf-mute education highly approved of by the Rev. Dr. McCaul, President of the University College, Toronto, and Dr. Howe, President of the Perkins Institution for the Blind, and the celebrated teacher of Laura Bridgman. This system of imparting instruction taxes to the utmost, the ingenuity of the teacher, Miss McGann, has in the discharge of her laborious duties given me much satisfaction.

In the year 1860 I received a valuable present of books from my dear co-laborer in Nova Scotia, Mr. J. Scott Hutton, Principal of the Halifax Institution, now of Belfast, Ireland.

At my suggestion the late Dr. Howe, of Boston, was invited by the committee to give an examination of his blind pupils, in order to press the claims and enlist the sympathy of the public for this afflicted class, as the following appeared in the minutes of the House of Assembly, 1856: "That an humble address be presented to His Excellency the Governor General, praying that information be laid before this House, as to what steps have been taken to carry into effect the law of this Province granting twenty thousand pounds for the erection of an institution for the deaf and dumb and for the blind in Upper Canada."

It may be well to mention here that eight or nine years before this, the Legislature voted eighty thousand dollars for this purpose.

In 1861 four blind pupils were received into the school. A teacher was engaged, and their instruction commenced under the direction of Dr. Morris, who had some previous experience.

In this year also, another lady teacher was engaged, a most noble girl, the late Miss Lizzie Hamilton.

In the year 1861 the Committee and officers were as follows:—

COMMITTEE,—The Hon. Vice Chancellor Spragge, The Hon. G. W. Allan, The Hon. S. B. Harrison, Rev. Dr. McCaul, Rev. Dr. Lillie, Rev. Dr. Green, Rev. H. J. Grasett, Rev. W. S. Darling, Rev. T. Ellerby, Rev. W. Reid, Rev. A. Topp, Rev. T. S. Kennedy, Rev. Dr. Jennings, Professor Kingston, Wm. McMaster, Esq., Dr. Ross, The Mayor, D. B. Read, Esq., Thomas Moss, Esq., Sheriff Jarvis, J. S. Howard, Esq., The Superintendent.

PRESIDENT,—Rev. Dr. McCaul.
VICE-PRESIDENT,—The Mayor.
SUPERINTENDENT,—B. R. Morris, M.D.
SECRETARY,—Rev. T. S. Kennedy.
TREASURER—William McMaster, Esq.
HEAD MASTER—J. B. McGann, Esq.

DEAF MUTE EDUCATION.

The terms of admission were to Day Pupils, twenty dollars per annum; boarders, one hundred and forty dollars per annum. The number of boarders was twenty one; day scholars, six.

The names of the pupils were as follows:—Alexander Paterson, Anthony Kirkpatrick, John Allen, John Johnson, Mary Cameron, Mary J. Rumley, Margaret Smith, Norman V. Lewis, William Cull, Archibald Campbell, Ellen J. Reid, Elexey J. Palmer, Sarah Snider, Agnes Baptie. John Hilker, John Longhead, Kezia Wheeler, Elizabeth Neeley, Matilda Hunter, James Dean, Jacob Zimmers,.

These twenty one deaf mute were all that could be provided for out of eighty six that applied for admission. It was a sad necessity that left the majority of this large number to pine away at home destitute of a training so necessary to their happiness, but the lack of funds stood in the way of doing anything further at that time.

The Committee on several occasions memorialized the Government for aid and in March, 1881, they thought it advisable to send the Superintendent to Quebec to urge the matter in person. His mission was so far successful that the grant was doubled.

The building then occupied was not very suitable and was also much crowded. The schoolroom was in a detached building at the rear with a boys' dormitory overhead, but the grounds were all that could be desired. The writer failed to find the old building, upon her last visit to Toronto. 490 Queen Street, West is no longer 490. New houses and stores have sprung up in bewildering numbers, many an old landmark has disappeared, and it is often difficult to locate a spot once the scene of our daily activity.

Several blocks of land at reasonable rates were offered to the society for a new building, which the state of the funds made it necessary to decline. It was also hoped that the Government would soon be aroused to the urgent claims for special provision presented by the large class of uneducated deaf mutes, many of whom were every year passing beyond the hope of improvement.

About this time the public schools began to be interested in the deaf and dumb; auxiliary societies were formed and large sums collected and sent in to the Treasurer. The Central School, Hamilton, heading the list with a collection of $97. This was very gratifying as the amount was raised by children anxious to extend the benefits of education so liberally bestowed upon themselves, to those not so favored.

In the Institution on Queen Street, the want of a resident male teacher was very much felt, but the funds would not guarantee this ex-

DEAF MUTE EDUCATION.

pense. Therefore after school hours the education of the boys was dropped and they wandered about idle and uncared for.

Mr. McGann says in his report for the year and in reference to the want of proper supervision after school hours:

"That the system pursued in our school has been highly successful in developing the reflective faculties of those committed to our care. I am happy to admit but that the measure of their attainments in the use of language as a communication with each other, has fallen short of the expectations I had formed. I cannot deny, and as you, Mr. President and gentlemen, are acquainted with, and cannot exercise control over, the hindrance which in some degree, operates injuriously against the better advancement of the pupils in colloquial forms of speech, and have done what in you lay to remedy the hindrance complained of. We must only hope for a brighter day to dawn on these "Children of Silence" who are the grateful recipients of your tender regard."

After this report was written the want of a supervisor became still more evident. The Superintendent anxious to make a large profit, supplied the boarders with food of the coarsest kind, ill cooked and on a limited scale. Nothing could arouse the displeasure of deaf mutes more, and goaded by the treatment which they received at the hands of one who neither understood them or had sympathy for them and left to themselves, they had every opportunity to plan all sorts of mischief. Several plots were discovered and nipped in the bud, others were perfected and carried out to an alarming extent. At last a plan to fire the school building was discovered, whereupon the society held an investigation into the management of the Institution, and withdrew their support. Dr. Morris now made advances to Mr. McGann to continue the school on their own responsibility, but Mr. McGann declined his offers and opened another school of his own on Little Richmond Street.

BROCK STREET SCHOOL, TORONTO.

DEAF MUTE EDUCATION.

LITTLE RICHMOND ST. SCHOOL

Very disheartening indeed were Mr. McGann's past experiences, yet encouraged by numerous kind friends in Toronto and through the country, and finding he had the confidence of the public, he put forth fresh efforts, and assisted by his two daughters visited the Country Councils and gave Public Examinations in different places. He was amply repaid, for the school was soon on a firmer footing than ever before, and so large was the number of pupils that he was obliged to rent another house, close by on Brock street, which was used as a dormitory for the boys.

The Public School Trustees granted the use of a large and pleasant schoolroom in the Phoebe Street School, where the teachers and their deaf mute pupils received every consideration from the other occupants of the building. The Head Master, Mr. Coyne and the Head Mistress, Miss Churchill taking much kindly interest in the work.

Dr. Morris continued his school in a vain endeavor to build it up. He procured the services of a deaf mute as teacher who was only partly educated and not very bright either. One by one the Country Councils withdrew their support and placed their beneficiaries under the charge of Mr. McGann. When the school closed for summer vacation in 1864 the number of his pupils had increased to 33, with applications for the admission of 30 more.

About this time Dr. Morris closed his school, sold part of the furniture and other movable property belonging to the trust, and soon afterward returned to England.

No report was issued from 1862 till June 30th, 1864, so the writer is at a loss for some little assistance to her memory. The amount of Dr. Morris' expenditure for 1862 was $6,160 with an accumulating debt of $1,300 not accounted for to the Treasurer. The total expenditure for that year was $7,460.69.

Under the heading of "Statement of the affairs of Asylums and Miscellaneous Charities" the following items appear as furnished to the Government for the year, 1863, by Dr. Morris:

"INCOME.

Received from Government			$1,600.00
"	"	Private Charity	00.00
"	"	Payments for Inmates	00.00
"	"	Other Income	00.00
		Total	$1,600.00

Expenditure $4,019.83
Nature of Governing Body.—None.

The Institution has undergone a change of management during the year.

No. of Inmates in the Institution at the beginning of the year...21
Admitted since 10
Discharged........................17
Remaining at end of year 14

The estimated number of days the whole have been in the Institution is 3,000, the cost of which is $4,019.83."

In a note to this report marked (*i*) it says that "The Report is not complete nor strictly correct. The Institution having undergone a change of management during the year, the number of days only is estimated."

At this time Mr. McGann had 33 pupils in charge at a cost of $1,173 for the half year.

The statement sent by Dr. Morris was incorrect especially as to numbers. There were 26 deaf mutes in attendance at the beginning of the year and 4 blind pupils. Twenty deaf mutes left the school that year.

DEAF MUTE EDUCATION.

Mr. McGann says in reference to the expenditure: "It may be well to remark in this connection, that during the time in which the late Superintendent managed the Institution not even one indigent mute or blind was supported free, except a vote of $60 for two years, to enable a wealthy merchant to educate his child. Of the $140 paid for each pupil the late Superintendent received $120 for the bare board of each pupil, and $10 each for contingent expenses; the remaining $10 was given me as school fees in addition to my salary of $800 per annum. Besides this he received $1,200 per annum salary, house with 4 acres of land attached, rent free, taxes paid, lighting and fuel provided, and every contingent met for him. This extravagant expenditure resulting in the closing of the Institution, leaving a debt of $2,800 or thereabouts to be liquidated; $2,000 of which was paid by the Government, and the sale by auction of the furniture of the Institution did not wipe out the balance of its indebtedness, as is evident from the fact that I received last year a bill from Jacques and Hay, amounting to $50 for furniture supplied to the Institution two years previously."

From the opening of the school in June, 1858, to January, 1860, Mr. McGann only received $640 for his laborious services. From July, 1863 to June, 1865, Mr. McGann received only $225 which he paid over to partly cover a sum he had borrowed to meet some requirements of the Institution. Surely the path of the pioneer was hard and never till after his death was any real acknowledgement made of his services. Mr. McGann himself says "Well might I say in my letter resigning my charge of Superintendency to another, that I have shifted from my shoulders a weight of anxious care, inconceivable to those who have never experienced the difficulties and trials which attend such a position." But he had not yet shifted the care, he carried it several years longer although greatly assisted by the enlarged Government grant and the increased interest throughout the country.

The names of the pupils attending Mr. McGann's school at the close of its last year in Toronto in 1864 were as follows:—

HEAD CLASS,—Anthony Kirkpatrick, William Baptie, Norman Lewis, Richard Slater, Mary J. Rumley, Hannah Preice.

SECOND CLASS,—Frank Cole, Edwin Pingle, John Allen, Benjamin Neely, John Johnson, Agnes Baptie, Mary Hurley.

THIRD CLASS. FIRST DIVISION,—John Moore, Duncan McKillop, Eliza Brown, Isabella Farley, George Bishop, Elizabeth Neely, Louisa Noyes.

DEAF MUTE EDUCATION.

SECOND DIVISION,—C. J. **Howe,** George Kelly, Thomas **Noyes,** James Jones, John Ellis, Robert **Foster,** Eliza Sloan, Charlotte **Noyes,** Louisa Noyes, Jane Foster, **Mary Farley,** Mary Neely.

Eli Bellmore, a blind young man, read Moore's type with fluency. He had learned the Boston, or square type, in the Flint School, Mich., for two years, and for six months read the Roman type at Dr. Morris' school. The deaf-mute girls, who were all grown up, did the whole work of the establishment in a very satisfactory manner. Mr. McGann says in the report for this year :

"I cannot close this report without the expression of my sincere thanks to the inhabitants of those towns where I gave examinations for the practical sympathy extended to my enterprise, and to the board of school trustees of this city for the use of a class room in the the Phoebe Street School-house, where I have received the benevolent co-operation of all the teachers. I feel truly grateful to you, Gentlemen (the Wardens of Counties) for the confidence reposed in me, more particularly Wm. Tyrrell, Esq., Warden of these United Counties, who from the foundation of the school has taken a warm interest in its welfare, and evinced a deep Christian sympathy for those unfortunate people whom the Almighty, in His inscrutable will, has created so helpless and dependent." Mr. Tyrrell is still living in Weston, Ontario, at a very advanced age. He was as Mr. McGann said,—"a kind friend to the deaf mutes." His hospitable home was always open to them and their teachers ; his warm friendship for the writer will never be forgotten.

DEAF MUTE EDUCATION.

FLORENCE BLOCK, HAMILTON.

In July, 1864, Mr. McGann was surprised by a visit from Dr. Ryall of Hamilton, who announced himself Medical Attendant of the Institution, and who requested the removal of the school to Hamilton. This was part of some political programme, and the removal was carried into effect, and Mr. McGann issued circulars notifying the pupils who were at their respective homes, of the change. Forty-seven deaf-mutes and six blind answered the call, and the school opened in the "Florence" Block, King Street, Hamilton, with a good augury of success, and with the addition of two teachers, Messrs. Terrill and Watson, (the latter is still engaged in the work of teaching the deaf at the Belleville Institute.) In respect to these gentlemen Mr. McGann states in his report for that year:—" The gentlemanly and courteous conduct of Messrs. Terrill and Watson, in the discharge of their onerous duties in the supervision of pupils, before and after school hours, combined with the tact displayed by them in conveying ideas to the minds of their deaf-mute pupils, bear evidence to their fitness for the responsible position which they occupy."

The house was in a very bad state of repair, and the assistance rendered by the boys of the Institution in painting, carpentry and glazing was most acceptable and gratifying. A row of stores under the building were repaired and utilized as class rooms, store rooms and kitchen.

DEAF MUTE EDUCATION.

fifty-four rooms were put in a state for occupation at Mr. McGann's own expense. A field containing half an acre of land was granted for a play ground by the owner, Ex-Mayor, McElroy, which was an act of kind consideration. Another field of two acres just above the Institution on King Street was rented and used as a garden.

In his reports Mr. McGann continually urged the Government to undertake the support and care of the Institution and in his last appeal remarks:—" The mothers of 800 deaf mutes cry aloud to the Executive Government to give their children the means by which they may have the power of expressing their thoughts and feelings and thus enable them to share in the intellectual enjoyment common to all, and know ' the length and breadth and depth of Christ's love which passeth knowledge.' The mothers of 600 blind supplicate the Executive Government for means to enable their unfortunates to bear the heavy burden consequent upon the loss of sight."

In another paragraph he states : " The boys have done in a workmanlike manner, one thousand, three hundred and eighty square yards of whitewashing, converted two thousand, eight hundred feet of lumber into school-room, dining-room, kitchen and store-room furniture, made a new roof over kitchen, containing eighteen square yards ; repaired and shingled roof over schoolroom, repaired 50 window sashes and 23 blinds, and put in 82 panes of glass. They have done the work for which a contract was put in for $600, the material of which cost but $70. The habits of industry thus promoted and the economy observed, will be productive of lasting benefits to the pupils." Truly the same spirit of industry has pervaded their lives, for wherever you find these old pupils, you will see evidences of thrift, industry and temperance to a high degree. Upon looking around at the well dressed people with their children who attended the First Convention held in Toronto in 1886, one who had been an old teacher could not but feel proud of the results.

The Blind were also receiving attention at this time, being taught for three hours daily by Mr. Terrill, in arithmetic, reading, writing, geography and history. A great want was felt for proper appliances and apparatus, but some very ingenious maps and slates were made by the teacher

Mr. Moon, of England, sent the munificent gift of 175 volumes for the library, which was indeed a boon to the Institution.

In the year 1866, a Board of Commissioners was appointed to visit and supervise the Institution, and the Government grant was doubled.

DEAF MUTE EDUCATION.

The removal to Dundurn was effected in 1857. Dundurn Castle was built by Sir Allan Macnab. When he died it was heavily mortgaged and fell into the hands of Hon. Samuel Mills. It was so large and so much out of repair that it was like a white elephant on his hands and he gladly rented it to Mr. McGann with the proviso that he was to put it into repair. The pupils did most of the repairing, so the cost was comparatively light. The committee appointed by the Government paid the rent out of the Government grant. Dundurn was afterwards sold to Mr. McInnes, who is the present owner. When Prince Alfred visited the Institution he said that Dundurn was an exact copy of the smallest of the Queen's palaces in England.

Dundurn with its ample grounds and beautiful scenery, generous fruit gardens, and luxurious flowers was a paradise for the deaf mutes. Nineteen County Councils contributed to the support of pupils, fifty-three of whom were in attendance. The amount of expenditure was

The Board consisted of the following gentlemen:—Chairman, Rev. W. Ormiston, D.D.; Rev. Egerton Ryerson, D.D., L.L.D., Chief Supt. of Education for Upper Canada; Mayor Magill, M.P.P,; Judge Logie; Ebenezer Stinson, Esq.; John McKeown, Esq. Secretary:—George Ryall, M.D.

Officers of the Institution:—

RESIDENT SUPERINTENDENT,—John B. McGann.
TEACHERS,—Joseph J. G. Terrill, James T. Watson, Miss H. McGann, and Miss Rumley.
MEDICAL SUPERINTENDENT,—George Ryall, M.D.
MATRON,—Miss Clark.

The maximum number of deaf mutes in attendance was 81, and of blind 10. Thus far no death had ever occurred in the Institution, and no serious case of illness, and this record was kept till the last day of school in Hamilton. This exemption from illness might be attributed to the constant care exercised to promote the comfort of the pupils, as regards heating the building, liberal diet and plenty of out-door exercise, with cheerful surroundings. Teachers and pupils formed a large and happy family circle.

Mr. McGann was most anxious for a separate Institution for the blind, and offered $200 as a subscription towards opening an Industrial Establishment in Hamilton where they could learn trades, but the work was dropped after the removal to Belleville until the Government created the Institute at Brantford.

DUNDURN CASTLE, HAMILTON.

DEAF MUTE EDUCATION.

$7,272, the Institution being entirely free from debt except $1,200 for salaries. The people of Hamilton continued their kindness to the pupils which was particularly evinced by the low prices charged them in their little shopping expeditions, in the large attendance at their exhibitions or entertainments, and in the goodly sums subscribed towards the maintenance of the Institution. The officials of the G.W.G. and the N.R. also granted free passes to the pupils proceeding home at the close of the schools.

The following is a copy of a letter written by one of the pupils, a semi-mute, who lost his hearing at seven years of age, and who was under instruction at this Institution for two years:

GALT, January 11th, 1868.

DEAR MISS McGANN,—I now commence to write a letter that ought to have been written long ago. I enjoyed myself very much at the Provincial Exhibition. You must excuse me for not calling on you before I left. I was so interested in the exhibition that I could not leave till it was time to go home. I only had one day at Christmas or I would have gone to Hamilton. It was a very quiet day with me, because I stayed at home. It has been a long time since I received a letter from David Hambly. I have had no skating this winter yet. Unless we have a change sleighing will be over and wheeled vehicles will be brought out again. I am attending a Russian doctor from Hamilton; he said he cured a deaf-mute there. I think I am getting a little better. He said it would take him about nine months to cure me. Perhaps you will know him. I have no more to say at present, but remain as ever yours truly,

R. S.

After the year 1868 no further reports were published, so that some rather important and interesting events were left unchronicled. Before the removal from Hamilton the death of Mr. J. J. G. Terrill took place at Dundurn. His loss was greatly mourned by the pupils to whom he was warmly attached. It had been intimated to him by John Sandfield Macdonald that he would be appointed Principal of the new Institution at Belleville which was then in course of erection, and at the express wish of Mr. McGann, who felt the weight of years and of past labours and responsibilities heavily pressing upon him. During his last illness the appointment was ratified but he never knew it. The following is the obituary of the *Hamilton Times*, written by the late Christopher Tyner, Esq.:—

DEAF MUTE EDUCATION.

"With deep regret we announce to-night the death of Mr. J. J. G. Terrill, one of the teachers in the Institution for the Deaf and Dumb. The shortness of his illness will make the announcement fall with heavy weight on the hearts of his many friends. For his friends were many and to all of them he was endeared by his sincerity and his quiet earnestness, his truthfulness and integrity, his kindly and unselfish disposition. Outside of his daily routine of teaching duty almost all his spare time was spent in ornithological pursuits and it was his enthusiasm in this study which led to his too early death. The science was a passion with him, and the hopes of a rare specimen to add to his valuable collection led him to incur hardships and fatigue which were too great for his strength. His name stands now, and will continue to stand very high among ornithologists of Canada; but the price paid is a very heavy one—a young life yielded up in the vigor of manhood, rich in its promises of future usefulness. With him is now over this fitful fever of life—happily with him a pure life, which has left behind it no recollections to be buried in forgetfulness, or thought of with a blush—a life so spent as to leave to those who remain nothing but pleasant and tender memories. To those who will hold their memories dearest, his widow and his children—all the comfort that human sympathy can afford will not be wanting."

In the spring of 1869 another removal was made as Dundurn was about to be sold. Two houses adjoining were procured on Main Street, Hamilton, but the accommodation was very limited; this was partly remedied by sending a class of deaf-mutes and the blind to Mrs. Terrill's residence, "Earlham Cottage," Emerald Street, but through the ignorance and carelessness of a deaf-mute boy, who placed some hot ashes in a pail in the stable, the place was burned to the ground on the 18th of May, the pupils barely escaping. If it had not been for the noble bravery of Miss M. McGann many might have lost their lives, as it was a most difficult task to get the frightened children out of their beds. One boy actually crept under his bed to hide himself.

The school closed at the vacation, never to open again in Hamilton. The services of Mr. McGann, Mr. Watson and the writer were transferred to the new Institution which opened the following October.

On the 20th of October, 1870, the Ontario Institution for the Deaf and Dumb was formally opened for the reception of pupils in the presence of His Excellency the Lieut.-Governor, the Honorable Attorney-General, the Honorable E. B. Wood, Treasurer, and other distinguished

DEAF MUTE EDUCATION.

MR. J. J. G. TERRILL.

EARLHAM COTTAGE.

BELLEVILLE INSTITUTION.

DEAF MUTE EDUCATION.

persons representing different sections of the Province. On that day the Principal and his staff of officers and teachers were installed in their respective offices by the Government Inspector, J. W. Langmuir, Esq. The officers and teachers were: J. W. Palmer, Principal; A. Christie, Bursar; Mrs. M. A. Keegan, Matron. Teachers—J. B. McGann, D. R. Coleman, S. T. Greene, Mrs. J. J. Terrill.

Only three pupils made their appearance, namely, Duncan Morrison, Arthur Bowen, and Mary Ettie Grace, but the number increased rapidly. Before the session ended there were 70 pupils in attendance. The number steadily increased from year to year.

When the doors were first opened the buildings were not quite completed and ready for occupation, and every thing was consequently in confusion. The management of the domestic affairs was seriously obstructed by the presence of the workmen in various parts of the building for a considerable time. The educational interests, however, steadily developed and progressed until they were in a satisfactory state. Towards the close of the first session, owing to the increasing number of pupils it was found necessary to appoint two additional teachers, viz., J. T. Watson and Miss Perry.

The buildings are beautifully located on the North Shore of the far-famed Bay of Quinte. The scenery in every direction and the healthiness of the place cannot be surpassed. There are now over two hundred and fifty pupils and thirteen teachers and twelve officers. Since the opening in 1870 there have been many changes and deaths among the officers and teachers. Mr. McGann died in 1880, and Dr. Palmer resigned as principal, and Mr. R. Mathison was appointed to the Superintendency in Sept. 1879.

The object of the Institution is to impart a general education as well as instruction in some professional or manual art to all deaf-mutes of both sexes between the ages of 7 and 20 residing in the Province of Ontario, and it is free to all but they must be sound in mind and body.

Mr. McGann's death took place on January 22nd, 1880, at his residence near the Institution. The chapel was draped with black, and his funeral took place from the Institution which he had founded. A graceful and modest tribute to his memory was erected by the deaf and dumb in the Belleville Cemetery. The last thought which strikes the writer and must fain be given is the remark of Dr. Workman:—" Pioneers are

DEAF MUTE EDUCATION.

often not merely unrewarded laborers but unpitied martyrs," and although at last Mr. McGann freely forgave his enemies for many acts of intolerance and unkindness, one cannot help thus simply recording it.

MAIN STREET SCHOOL, HAMILTON.

INSCRIPTION:

Sacred

TO THE MEMORY OF

JOHN B. McGANN,

PIONEER OF DEAF-MUTE EDUCATION IN CANADA.

DIED

JANUARY 22nd, 1880

IN HIS 69th YEAR.

———o———

ERECTED BY THE DEAF AND DUMB OF
ONTARIO, CANADA.

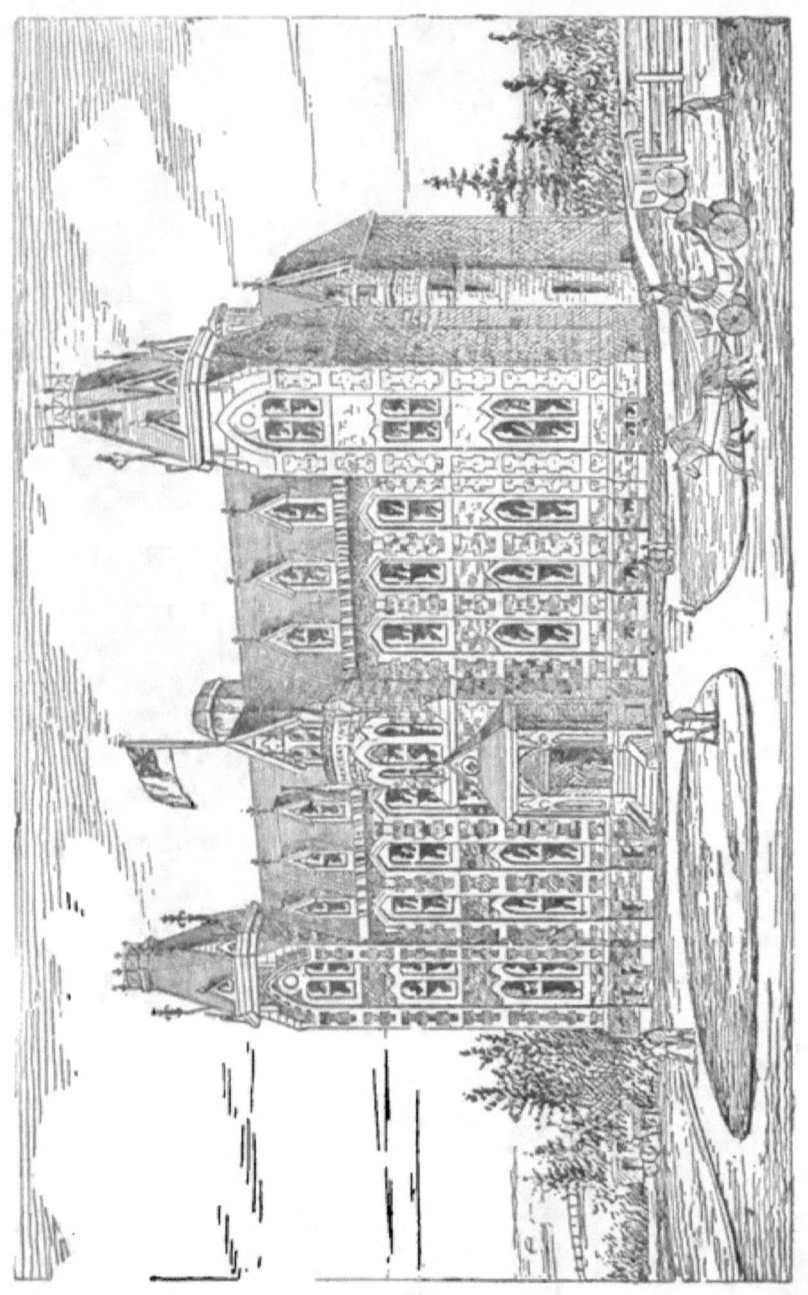

MACKAY INSTITUTION.

DEAF MUTE EDUCATION.

HISTORY OF THE PROTESTANT INSTITUTION FOR DEAF-MUTES, MONTREAL.

In compiling an historical sketch of the educational establishment for the Protestant deaf-mutes of Lower Canada, it may not be out of place first to take a glance at the state of deaf-mute instruction in the Dominion of Canada when the writer took up his residence at Montreal in the year 1868.

At that period there were four institutions to meet the educational requirements of some 3,500 deaf-mutes scattered over the Dominion, viz.: The two Roman Catholic Institutions at Montreal; the Nova Scotia Institution at Halifax; the Upper Canada Institution at Hamilton. The former were the oldest, having been founded in the year 1848, under the patronage of the Roman Catholic Bishop of Montreal and the Seminary of St. Sulpice (the most powerful and wealthy Roman Catholic corporation in America.) One of these Roman Catholic Institutions is for boys, and the Rev. A. Belanger is the principal. The other is for girls, and is conducted by the nuns. The Institution at Halifax was established in August, 1856, and has ever since been most ably and successfully conducted by Principal Hutton. The institution in Upper Canada was begun at Toronto in 1858 by Mr. J. B. McGann, who may be regarded as the pioneer of deaf-mute instruction in the western part of the Dominion. In 1868, Mr. McGann was struggling manfully to save his school from hopeless bankruptcy and ruin. The education of deaf-mutes was a new departure to the sturdy pioneers of that period in Western Canada. Some there were who admitted the importance of educating deaf-mutes, but doubted its possibility; others had no objection to the trial being made, but protested against being taxed to support "dummies" while at school. The writer could not help sympathizing with Mr. McGann when he said, "I am obliged to buy my fuel on credit, and keep a pass-book with my grocer and baker. My furniture has been twice distrained for rent and taxes." Mr. McGann's spare moments were occupied in diffusing information respecting the deaf and dumb, and in convincing the public that their education was not only possible but absolutely necessary. This, coupled with many examination tours, had the desired effect. The Government of Ontario came to Mr. McGann's assistance, and in 1870 opened the present noble Institution at Belleville, under the direction of R. Mathison, Esq.

It will thus be seen that provision was made for the education of

DEAF MUTE EDUCATION.

deaf-mutes in the western part of the Dominion, in the Maritime Provinces, and for the Roman Catholic deaf-mutes in Lower Canada; but nothing had been done for deaf-mutes of the English-speaking population, or Protestants, in Lower Canada. Many of these were the descendants of the early settlers, the United-Empire loyalists. None of their deaf-mutes had received any instruction, except in one or two cases, where the parents possessed sufficient means to send them to Hartford or to England for instruction. The writer had not been long a resident in Canada's commercial capital before the necessity of a school for Protestant deaf-mutes was forcibly brought to his notice by the father of one of them, who appealed with sorrowful heart on behalf of his grown-up deaf-mute son, totally uninstructed. Others were soon discovered, some of school age and some past the prime of manhood and womanhood, with no school in the whole Province where their parents could have them taught according to their own religious belief. The writer saw a new field of labour opened for him. His experience for some years as an assistant under the late Dr. Baker, of the Yorkshire Institution for Deaf-Mutes, and as a missionary to adult deaf-mutes in different parts of England, amply fitted him for a career of usefulness, although surrounded by very great difficulties. A long correspondence on the subject of a school for Protestant deaf-mutes in Lower Canada took place in the Montreal Daily Witness. Information respecting the numbers of deaf-mutes in the Province was diligently sought for; influential Protestant gentleman engaged in commerce, science, and education were consulted, and their aid asked for and obtained. There were no reliable returns of vital statistics published for the Province, and the public seemed to know no more about deaf-mutes and deaf-mute instruction than they did in Ontario when Mr. McGann began his uphill labors. Many doubted the writer's deaf-dumbness on account of the easy way he handled the English language and his literary productions. But it was at last ascertained, as near as could be, that there was about 3,500 deaf-mutes in the Dominion, some 1,300 being in Lower Canada; and, judging by the relative proportions of Protestant and Roman Catholic populations in the Province, there were probably 200 Protestant deaf-mutes, and of these about 75 were of school age, viz., between 7 and 25 years.

The information thus gathered and the knowledge on the subject of deaf-mute education possessed by the writer were published in the Witness. More correspondence ensued, and several applicants for edu-

canon were recieved by the writer. Further inquiry revealed the fact that the provincial legislature of Lower Canada before confederation had voted $80,000 for purposes of education of deaf-mutes, but this sum has not yet been paid out, and the record will probably be all that will now remain in connection with it.

During this correspondence in the public prints, which lasted more than a year, (1868 to 1869,) many of the benevolent Protestants in the city of Montreal, ever alive to the wants of suffering humanity, were quietly watching the issue, and taking notes of the facts brought to light. A few of the most prominent of them came forward and took up the subject. Mr. McGann, then principal of the Ontario Institution at Hamilton, was invited to Montreal to give an exhibition of the progress of some of his pupils, and an address on the subject of deaf-mute instruction ; this took place at the close of 1868.

On the 7th of January, 1869, a **public meeting** of those interested in the good work took place in Montreal, and the following prominent Protestant citizens formed themselves into a society to establish an educational institution for Protestant deaf-mutes in Lower Canada :

Ladies.—Mesdames Andrew Allan, P. Redpath, J. W. Dawson, (McGill University,) Major, Bond, Cramp, Fleet, Moffatt, Brydges, Browne, Workman.

Gentlemen.—Charles Alexander, (president,) Thomas Cramp, (vice-president,) Fred. Mackenzie, (hon. sec-treas.,) Thos. Workman, John Dougall, (proprietor of the Montreal Witness,) Wm. Lunn, G. Moffatt, J. A. Matthewson, J. H. R. Moloon, Hon. J. J. C. Abbott, E. Carter, Q. C., P. D. Browne, W. H. Benyon, I. F. Barnard, John Leeming, and S. J. Lyman.

With this influential committe great and rapid progress was made, and next day, January 8, another meeting was held. It was resolved to ask for legislative aid and a charter, and to appeal for public subscriptions. Mr. Mackenzie, the secretary-treasurer, reported that he had made diligent inquiries respecting the probable number of Protestant deaf-mutes in the Province, and believed there were over 2,000. The committe resolved to rent a suitable house and grounds.

At this juncture, Mr. W. H. Vanvliet, mayor of Lacolle, some 40 miles south of Montreal, made an offer to the committe of their choice of three splendid sites for the proposed Institution. Any of these lots would make a very generous donation to any charitable institution ; but the committe thought that to remove the Institution so far away

DEAF MUTE EDUCATION.

would deprive it of the contributions from the benevolent of Montreal, its main source of support.

On the 19th January, 1869, another meeting was held, at which it was reported that the handsome sum of $5,950 had been subscribed, and more was promised. The principal collector of this large sum was Mr. Thomas Cramp, the vice-president; the other members of the committee, being otherwise engaged, could not then assist in collecting, or the amount would doubtless have been much larger.

The work of the hon. secretary-treasurer was no sinecure. He sent out hundreds of circulars to ministers in all parts of the Province to obtain the number, age, sex, circumstances, etc., of all Protestant deaf-mutes of the Province. It may be of interest to the profession to learn how far the circulars succeeded in this mixed community, where the Protestants form only a small minority of the population.

On the 26th January, 250 circulars to Protestant ministers had brought twenty-three replies, reporting only five deaf-mute and five blind Protestants.

On the 10th March it was stated that 112 replies to circulars had been received, reporting 38 deaf-mutes, 8 of school age; of 34 blind returned only 5 were of school age. More circulars were sent out.

On April 30, 210 replies were recieved, reporting 57 deaf-mutes, 35 males and 22 females. Their ages were: Between 16 and 21 years, 8 males and 5 females, in all 13; between 21 and 30 years, 8, being 4 of each sex.

The committee now wished to know—
1. Between what ages can deaf-mutes be educated?
2. Whether both sexes should be educated together?
3. Whether the blind and deaf-mutes should be educated together?

These questions were submitted to several experts, including the writer. All recommended the education of the sexes together, but advised a separate school for the blind, and named the ages at which deaf-mutes could be educated as from 7 to 25 years.

On the 15th December, 1869, another meeting of the committee was held, which the late Rev. Collins Stone of Hartford attended by invitation. He expressed pleasure and satisfaction with his interview with the writer and his testimonials, and recommended them to make a trial with a small school under the management of the writer, with his wife as matron. He kindly offered to the writer and his wife to spend a few months in the Hartford Institution to acquire a knowledge of the

system of instruction, if necessary. He continued to be a warm friend of the Institution up to the time of his lamented death, which took place a few months after his visit to Montreal.

On the 4th May, 1870, another meeting of the committe was held, and it was unanimously resolved **that the writer should at** once look for a suitable **house and grounds, and open school in September.** A house, with ample **grounds, in a very healthy locality, just out**side of the **city limits. (Cote St. Antoine,) was obtained in July,** at an annual rental of **$400, with** option of **purchase within five years for $8,000, the extent of ground** being 58,080, **square feet. The house** contained accommodation **for** about 20 pupils, **but** very scant **provision** for teachers. The **double** doors of the parlor **were** removed, and the room was **used as school-room,** chapel and sitting-room for the pupils. Baths were **put in and few** alterations made, in order that we might make the best **of the** small accommodation the house afforded.

At this meeting **the** committee learned that their attempt to obtain leglislative aid for the school had failed, but they were not discouraged, and made another application for a grant, feeling they had the same right to aid from the State as their Roman Catholic fellow-citizens had for their Institution. The goverment at last made the Institution a grant of $1,000, which has since been **increased to $**1,729.

On the **1**5th September, 1870, the Protestant Intitution for Deaf-Mutes opened **its** doors, **for the** first time, for the reception of pupils. During **that** month and the following October, 11 pupils, 9 boys and 2 girls, **were** admitted. Of these **six** paid full fees, ($90,) **and** five were free.

On the 1st November, 1870, the Institution was formally opened **to the public by the** Protestant **Bishop** of Montreal and Metropolitan of **Canada, in the** presence of **a** large assemblage of prominent ladies and **gentlemen, and** another charitable institution was added **to the long list for which** Montreal is famous.

During the first session **of** the new school sixteen pupils **were** admitted, **thirteen boys** and three girls, one of the latter being a young woman **deaf, dumb,** and blind. **She** was in a most deplorable **state.** Her condition was enfeebled by **long** confinement and neglect, and, **at** times, she **was subject to** fits of ungovernable temper ; at other times she would show signs of great intellect, and some progress was made in learning the manual alphabet, with the aid of raised letters, which were procured for her benefit. After being a few weeks **in** the Institution **she was a**ble to communicate her wants in signs, **and** could go about

the house unaided. Her health, however, began to fail, and her **parents** contemplating a removal to the West, and it being found **that the Institution in its early infancy had** not the necessary accommodation and staff **of** teachers which her case required, her parents were desired to remove her.

The numerous **duties which** devolved **upon the principal and** matron were such as to **require** all their **time and constant care from** early morning till late **at** night. Eight hours **a day for six days a week** were spent in the school-room; three hours **a day were devoted to teaching** different kinds **of** work about the place, **and to training the pupils in** habits of industry. Many a night **the principal had to sit at his desk** attending to correspondence, and **the monthly accounts and reports for** the meetings **of the** board of directors. It was, indeed, **a year of real hard work, care,** and anxiety. The matron, with the **aid of a single** female cook and the two girls, did all **the** domestic work of **the Institution,** and took upon herself the instruction of the classes **of pupils of a** low grade of intellect. The principal taught two classes **and the drawing-class** after school hours, besides acting as teacher of **trades, steward, and** supervisor. On Sundays a Sabbath-school was held, **and three hours were** devoted to religious **instruction** by means of the sign-language.

The system of instruction in this Instiuttion is, to a very great extent, similar to that adopted by the Nova Scotia Institution **at** Halifax Natural signs, writing, and the manual alphabet (both single and double handed) are the chief instruments depended on for teaching. In so small a school great diversity of intellect prevailed, which rendered it necessary to divide the pupils into several classes, and the ingenuity of the teacher was taxed to the utmost to devise methods of reaching the dormant minds of the pupils. Some of our friends suggested that the articulation method as carried on in the excellent school at Northampton, Massachusetts, should be adopted in this Institution, but they soon saw that with such pupils it was an impossibility. The object persistently kept prominently in view during the **whole** session of the first year and ever afterwards, has been to give the deaf-mute a knowledge of language (written or otherwise) by whatever methods long experience has suggested as the best and most certain, and to **inculcate** habits **of** industry, with moral and religious training.

The public interest in the success of the Institution during the first **year was very** great, especially towards the close of the session; visitors

were numerous, almost daily, which obliged the principal to leave his classes to show them about the place and answer their questions by the slow process of writing; but the good work was perseveringly continued until the day arrived for the first public examination of the pupils, which was held in the Mechanics' Hall in Montreal on the 13th June, 1871, and was presided over by J. W. Dawson, LL.D., F.R.S., principal of the McGill University. There was a very large audience present, including many of the most prominent men of the city. As this was our first appearance before the public, and many drawbacks had attended the session just closed, the teachers and pupils felt no small distrust as to the result of their labors. They were, however, so kindly received and assisted by the president of the Institution (Charles Alexander), that they were encouraged to do their best on the occasion, which was attended with great success. At the close of the examination, Dr. Dawson asked the audience to adopt a written recognition of the services rendered by the teachers, and their thorough approval of the system of instruction adopted by the Institution. This proposal was heartily approved by the audience, and the chairman drew up the following words, read them to the audience, and presented them to the writer:

" The audience desire me to say that they are very much gratified with what they have seen, and desire to encourage you in your good work, and to express their approval of the pupils.

PRINCIPAL DAWSON."

An examination tour through the Province was now resolved on. The secretary-treasurer, F Mackenzie, Esq., accompanied by the principal and two of the advanced pupils, visited the largest Protestant towns in the Province, and held public meetings and examinations of the pupils at each place. At all of these places the greatest interest in the work was shown by the public. Collections to defray expenses were taken up at the close of each examination. A very enthusiastic reception was given us at Quebec city, where three of the pupils resided and took part in the examinations. A subscription was immediately taken up to provide the Institution with a printing press and founts of type by a few friends in Quebec, and the handsome sum of $267.53 was handed to the secretary-treasurer.

During the following session Miss Clara Bulmer was engaged as an assistant teacher, and to instruct semi-mutes in articulation, which relieved Mrs. Widd, the matron, of her duties in the school-room, and enabled her to devote all her time to her own family and the domestic

cares of the Institution. A carpenter was engaged to instruct the boys in the use of carpentry tools, and the teaching of printing was undertaken by the principal. The reports of the Institution and other matters were executed by the boys after school hours.

The first session of eight hours daily in the school-room having proved too exhaustive for the teachers and too wearisome to the pupils, the time in school was reduced to five hours for five days a week, and an hour a day was given to articulation with three or four promising pupils, and an hour twice a week was devoted to drawing. This change speedily showed beneficial results. The health of the pupils and teachers improved, and their intellectual progress continued to be quite as satisfactory as previously.

On the 20th January, 1873, the Governor-General of Canada, Lord Dufferin, and Lady Dufferin visited the Institution, and conversed with the pupils in the double-handed alphabet, much to their delight and surprise.

The board of managers felt the urgent need of larger and better premises for the Institution, as every year since the first public examination the number of pupils admitted into the small house used by the Institution exceeded 20, and on one occasion there were no less than 27, besides the principal, matron, assistant teacher, and two domestic servants, crowded together in the building, which could only comfortably accommodate 15 at most! Many applications for admission were refused or postponed. The difficulties of the board of managers in raising funds to meet current expenses were very great, the Institution having to depend for support on public subscriptions, the fees of paying pupils, and the $1,000 grant made by the provincial legislature, which all together were never sufficient to keep the Institution from debt by current expenses. The salaries of the teachers (principal and matron included) did not exceed $600 a year, and the utmost economy and frugality were practised in all expenditures. Still, the finances of the Institution continued in rather an unsatisfactory state. The managers tried from time to time to raise funds for enlarging the building, or to buy more land and build elsewhere. One lady manager, Mrs. C. J. Brydges, whose active benevolence is well known in Canada, managed with no small trouble to collect $2,061 towards a building fund, and others of the board of managers exerted themselves in the same direction; but not much success attended their efforts on account of great finincial depression at the time.

DEAF MUTE EDUCATION.

The census returns of Lower Canada were published in 1873-4, and showed a total of 1,669 deaf-mutes—883 males and 786 females; but every attempt to find the number of those who were of Protestant parentage failed, and these returns proved of comparatively little value to the Institution. New cases of Protestant deaf-mutes continued to be reported to the principal and president of the Institution, but nothing particularly was done to induce them to enter the Institution on account of its financial condition and the want of proper accommodation.

Matters became worse in 1876, when failures in trade and financial depressions were universal. The Institution was without funds and much in debt. The prospects of a larger building and better times were to all appearance as far off as ever. The managers felt much discouraged, and to keep the Institution going the secretary-treasurer and the president advanced money from their private funds. As the dark cloud gathered over the prospects of the future of the Institution, and "while we were trying," as the worthy president of the Institution stated at the last annual meeting, "to make both ends meet, in the time of our great anxiety God raised up a friend to help us in the very way we wished—that is, to extend our efforts by means of a larger building—and put it into the heart of an old and respected fellow-citizen, Joseph Mackay, Esq., to give us a splendid piece of land, and to erect thereon at his own expense a stone building capable of accommodating 80 pupils and their teachers."

The corner-stone of this magnificent gift was laid on the 6th June, 1877, in the presence of a large number of ladies and gentlemen, on which occasion this kind and Christan friend of the deaf and dumb—who will ever keep his name in grateful remembrance—addressed the large assembly as follow :

"MR. CHAIRMAN, LADIES AND GENTLEMEN : The Institution for which this building is being erected has had as yet a brief career of usefulness. Among its founders and friends may be numbered leading citizens of Montreal, besides ladies and gentlemen, and I think special mention should be made in this connection of our worthy chairman, Mr. Charles Alexander ; our secretary, Mr. Frederick Mackenzie ; Mr. Thomas Cramp, Mr. Andrew Allen, Mr. Dougall, senior, who is always doing good wherever he goes, Mr. Widd, the principal of the school, as well as the governors and managers, who have done good work. The work of the school was commenced in 1870, with sixteen pupils ; the largest number yet in attendance was twenty-five, during the session of

DEAF MUTE EDUCATION.

1874 and 1875. The total number connected with the school from its formation is forty-one; some of these have continued through several sessions, and others have remained for only a few months. Of the twenty-two in attendance last session, seven have paid full fees, five partial fees, and ten were free pupils. Of the education given, it may be sufficient for me to say that it is under the able and judicious direction of the principal and his assistants, and embraces intellectual and spiritual culture, as well as instruction in several of the useful arts of life. The pupils are prepared, when they remain a sufficient time in the Institution, to make their way in this world, and have their minds and hearts turned to the higher realities of the world to come. What a blessing to the afflicted! And thus the founders and supporters are made a blessing, as stewards of God's bounty. The goverment of our Province has given a small annual grant in aid of the Institution, but its support has been chiefly drawn from private benevolence. Feeling deeply the importance and value of the work done, and wishing to promote its success and extension, I resolved some time ago, as announced in a letter addressed to you, Mr. Chairman, on the 24th of November last, to erect this building, and to place it and the grounds attached to it in the hands of trustees, to be used by them and their successors for the education of the Protestant deaf and dumb of this Province. Several conversations with Mr. Widd, who spoke of the immediate necessity of larger buildings, and the difficulties in obtaining funds led, to this decision, specially when on mentioning it to a relative, the reply was 'Why not do it yourself?' I only add, that I trust and pray this building may be completed without any accident or untoward incident, and be carried to a speedy and successful completion; and for years and generations to come the Institution may, through the Divine favor, prove a source of manifold blessings to the afflicted class whose good it seeks, and may never lack generous, warm-hearted friends, and wise and godly instructors to carry on the work."

The board of managers have resolved, as a token of their gratitude to Mr. Mackay for his noble gift, to change the name of the Institution to "The Mackay Institution for Protestant Deaf-Mutes." The new Institution is expected to be ready for occupation in the fall of 1877. It is being erected on one of the most picturesque sites on the Island of Montreal, commanding a view of the St. Lawrence, the mountain, being visible from so many points, being situated on Cote St. Luc road. It was originally intended to erect a building to accommodate about 50

pupils, but after much careful thought and study Mr. Mackay decided to construct a much larger building, to accommodate from 80 to 100. The style of the building is Gothic, having four facades of rock-faced courses, with trimmings and openings, water-table belts, courses, and bands of cut stone. The building will be 95 by 50, and three stories in height, having a well-elevated basement and mansard roof, ornamented. There are two towers, one at each end, and the main entrance is in the centre, with a handsome flight of stone steps, portico, etc. The basement is 10 feet high; the floor being level with the ground, will afford abundance of light and air. There are three entrances; one on the north side for baker, butcher, etc., and one for the girls and one for the boys to the play-ground, with doors opening into the hall and wide corridor, and refectory 43 by 20, with openings on three sides, with serving-room, teachers' dining-room, kitchen, scullery, laundry, larder, cook's pantry, store-rooms, lavatories, fuel cellar, and two boilers for heating the building with hot water. The ground floor will be 15 feet high, and will contain an octagonal vestibule 12 feet in diameter, opening to a hall 20 by 14, having a handsome staircase six feet in width in the centre, and two returns of four feet. On the left are two rooms, a class-room 37.7 by 25, and the boys' recreation-room 37.6 by 16. Both these rooms can be made one for meetings, etc., by sliding the doors out of the way which divide them. On the right is the office and board-room, with safe, 16.6 by 16, and teacher's room, 18 by 16, and corridor between them, with staircase and private entrance leading into the girls' recreation-room in front, 20 by 16, and in rear a class-room 19 by 16. The second story will be 12 ft. 6 in. high, and will contain a library 18 by 12, two bedrooms or dormitories, each 16 by 16, and ten bedrooms, each 11 by 26; girls and boys' lavatories, hall in the centre, with corridor 8 ft. in width; and staircase at each end. The third story will be 12 ft. 6 in. high, and will contain dormitories, hospitals, and lavatories, nurse's room, galleries, etc. To secure through ventilation and warming, the ventilating and smoke flues, each 3 by 2 ft., are carried up through the centre of the building, with register at the floor and ceiling on each story. The heating apparatus will consist of two of Spence's hot-water boilers, connected so that they can be worked separate or together, with coils in all the rooms, halls, corridors, dormitories, etc. The work, which is of the most substantial character, was designed and is being carried out under the superintendence of John James Browne, a Montreal, architect.

DEAF MUTE EDUCATION.

THOMAS WIDD.

Mr. Thomas Widd is a Yorkshireman. He was born on the 4th of August, 1839, at Driffield, on the East coast of Yorkshire. His ancestors have lived and died there from time immemorial and were engaged in agriculture and horticulture. He is the only one of the family that has ventured to leave old England to reside abroad. He lost his hearing at the age of three years by a severe attack of scarlet fever, which left him on the verge of the grave for a long time. For many months after losing his hearing he was a helpless invalid. When sufficiently recovered he was sent to a public school, but the learned "pedagogue," mistaking his deafness for obstinacy, caned him tremendously and turned him out of the school. He remained at home till he was thirteen years old, during which time his father made every effort to have his hearing restored. Every known remedy was resorted to and every aurist from near and afar was consulted, but without the least effect. In 1852 he was sent to the Yorkshire Institution for Deaf-mutes at Doncaster. To

DEAF MUTE EDUCATION.

him this school was like a new world, and he made very rapid progress in acquiring knowledge. Previous to being sent to Doncaster his father had taught him the Delgarno alphabet and had succeeded in giving him some knowledge by writing in the air with his finger. While at Doncaster he was partly instructed by the Rev. S. Smith, now the Chaplain of the Royal Association for Deaf-mutes, and by Mr. Alexander Melville, the Principal of the Llandaff School for Deaf-mutes, Wales. Under these good teachers and Christian men Mr. Widd made great advance, and when he left school, after being there only 18 months, he was in the highest class. When he returned home he had acquired a very strong taste for reading, and every book in his father's house and all he could borrow or buy were diligently perused and throughly studied. This taste for books has clung to him through life, and has enabled him to store his mind with a large amount of practical knowledge and to acquire a good command of the English language. After being at home some time thus employed, he was engaged as assistant engineer in a large steam sawmill in his native town. He soon learned the duties necessary to fit him to take entire charge of the powerful engine and the machinery which drove all the circular and other saws in the mill. It was a very dangerous occupation, especially for a deaf-mute; but he gave his employer such satisfaction that entire confidence was reposed in him. Dr. Baker, the principal of the Yorkshire Institution, on learning of the nature of Mr. Widd's occupation, visited him and persuaded him to accept a position as assistant teacher and printer in the Institution, where he would run less risk to life and limb and have a chance to continue his studies and learn a profession and a trade at the same time, he accepted this offer and underwent the usual training of a teacher and learned printing. All the teachers trained by Mr. Baker have distinguished themselves more or less as principals or masters of the professions. Dr. Baker's training was of a Spartan character. No matter what he required being done, whether to dig a ditch, paper a wall, print or teach, they had to obey and ask no questions. Their pay was meagre, and the fare of the plainest; and they slept in the pupil's dormitories. After being several years under this kind of discipline, Mr. Widd was invited to organize and establish the Sheffield Deaf-mute Association, which he undertook to do and resigned his position in the Institution. Several other gentlemen had previously attempted this work, but without success. Their chief places of resort were certain taverns whose landlords had learned their signs and the manual alphabet to allure them to

DEAF MUTE EDUCATION.

their bars, where they spent most of their money. Mr. Widd being acquainted with several of the deaf-mutes, sought them out and succeeded in calling a mass meeting outside of the taverns and laid before them his scheme for an association for their mutual benefit and improvement. Mr. Widd had no pecuniary inducement in this work; it was one of love and self-sacrifice. About sixty adult deaf-mutes resided then in Sheffield and nearly all of them consented to enroll themselves to form the association. Mr. Widd rented a large hall in the central part of the town, paying the rent for the first quarter in advance out of his own pocket. After nine months faithful missionary work in this town a great change was to be seen in the deaf-mutes. Nearly all had signed the pledge, married and established comfortable houses. The religious service were well attended as also were the week-day lectures. The association has since grown and prospered, and they are now building a church of their own in the town. After getting this society established Mr. Widd assisted in starting others and encouraging those already commenced in different parts of England. He supported himself during the time by working as a printer and by writing for the press. The only compensation he received for his labor among the deaf-mutes was a handsome writing-desk with a suitable inscription engraved on the lid, expressing the gratitude of the Sheffield deaf-mutes for the services rendered them. Mr. Widd married Miss Margaret Fitzakerly, also an old pupil at the Yorkshire Institution, on the 1st January, 1864, which proved to be a very happy union. They had four children, one being born in London, and the others in Montreal. In September, 1867, Mr. Widd came to Ontario, where his wife's father lives on a farm, and continued his labors among the Canadian deaf-mutes. He brought with him excellent recommendations from the Rev. S. Smith, Alex. Melville and many others. When he visited Hamilton, the late M. McGann received him kindly and promised him a position on the teaching staff of the new Ontario Institution then about to be established at Belleville. He next proceeded to Montreal and found a warm friend in Mr. John Dougall, the proprietor and founder of the Montreal Witness, who employed him on that paper and the New Dominion Monthly. To both of the publications he contributed numerous articles on various topics. He had not been long in Montreal before he saw that the Protestant deaf-mutes of the province of Quebec needed a school, and he lost no time in taking measures to have one established for them. The results of his labors is seen in the noble Institution of which he

DEAF MUTE EDUCATION.

was principal, and which was donated to the deaf-mutes of the Province of Quebec by Mr. Joseph Mackay. A full history of this Institution, written by Mr. Widd and authorized by the board of managers was put in the American Annals of the Deaf and Dumb for 1877.

FIRST PROTESTANT DEAF-MUTE SCHOOL IN MONTREAL.

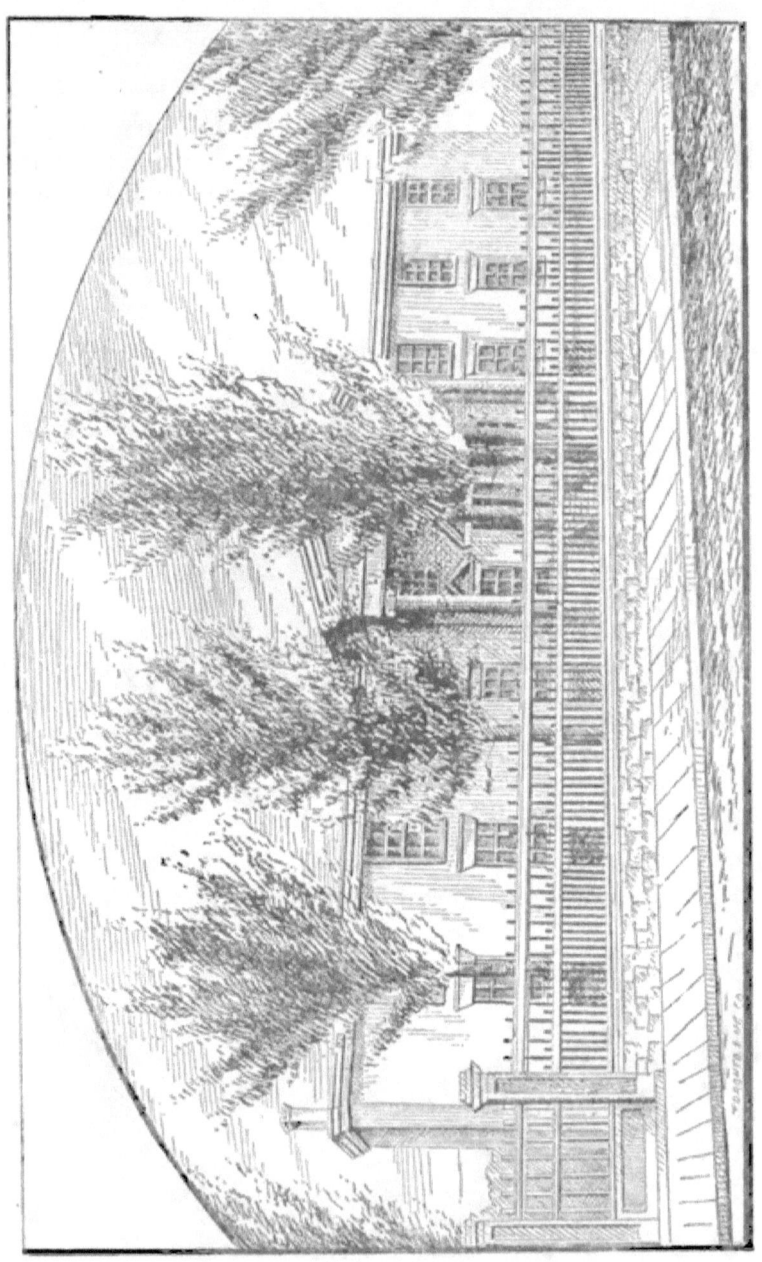

HALIFAX INSTITUTION.

HISTORY OF DEAF-MUTE EDUCATION IN NOVA SCOTIA.

Looking at the 800 or 900 deaf-mutes scattered over the Provinces of Nova Scotia and New Brunswick, Prince Edward Island and Newfoundland, who by their misfortune are excluded from the precious opportunities of instruction, and of moral and social improvement, enjoyed by others, two questions naturally arise. 1. How many of these are susceptible of education?, and 2. What has been done to ameliorate their condition?

In answer to the first of these queries, taking our experience in Nova Scotia as a fair standard, we presume it would not be overstepping the mark to suppose that 18 or 20 per cent. of the whole—about 150 individuals—ought this moment to be at school, sharing the education, formerly monopolized, so to speak, by their more favored hearing and speaking fellow countrymen, advantages to which they are surely entitled by every consideration of justice and humanity.

The answer to the second question may be said to be embraced in the history of the Halifax Institution for the Deaf and Dumb—the only regular establishment of the kind within the limits of the Maritime Provinces. Twenty years ago there was no provision within their bounds for the education of the hundreds of mutes, who with scarcely an exception, were utterly destitute of instruction—passing through life in a condition of the saddest mental and moral darkness—ignorant alike of their nature, their duty and their destiny. In a few instances Legislative aid had enabled parents to send their mute children to the States for the instruction unattainable at home, but how little was accomplished in this way may be seen from the fact, that, during the long period of fifty years, the whole number of mutes received into the Hartford Asylum, from the British Provinces was only twenty-five; and of these not more than six were supported by the Provincial Legislatures. Of the twenty-five, 11 were from Nova Scotia, 5 from Canada East, 5 from Canada West, and 4 from New Brunswick. Some Provincial deaf-mutes may have been educated during that period at other Institutions in the States besides Hartford, and a few certainly—two at least from Nova Scotia—in the schools of the mother country, but in all probability, the entire number of British American mutes who had enjoyed the blessing of education, since the commencement of the century, would not exceed thirty or forty.

It is worthy of note that of the whole number of mutes from the British Provinces mentioned as receiving instruction in the Hartford

DEAF MUTE EDUCATION.

School, previous to the opening of institutions for their benefit, nearer home and on their own soil, nearly one-half were from one of the smaller, less populous, and least known—though by no means the least important colony—the Province of Nova Scotia. There is also reason to believe that the six, stated to have been supported by the Provinces, were all beneficiaries of the Legislature of Nova Scotia.

These circumstances, while indicative of an earlier awakening to the claims of the Deaf and Dumb than in the more populous and wealthy sister provinces, are also in harmony with the interesting fact that the earliest advocate of deaf-mute education on the American continent, author of the work entitled "Vox Oculis Subjecta" published in London in 1783, giving an account of Braidwood's school in Edinburgh,—if not by birth a Nova Scotian, was yet identified with this Province both by education and official position for many years, being engaged in military duty in Halifax and other parts of the Province, previous to the outbreak of the Revolutionary war, and subsequently, holding the position of High Sheriff of Halifax County About the beginning of this century, Mr. Green was residing in Medford, Mass., where he appears to have devoted his leisure hours to advocating in the journals the importance of educating the deaf and dumb, and endeavoring to enlist public sympathy in their behalf. Some of his articles may be found in the Boston papers, particularly the New England Palladum for the year 1793. The first attempt at an enumeration or census of the deaf-mutes of Massachusetts and the United States was also due to Mr. Green's instrumentality.

His son, Charles Green, the first educated deaf-mute of American birth, was a pupil of Braidwood, in his articulating school in Edinburgh from 1780 to 1786, and, according to his father's account in the "Vox Oculis Subjecta," attained remarkable proficiency both in articulate speech and in scholarship. This young man was unfortunately drowned shortly after completing his education while shooting wildfowl on Cole Harbor in the neighborhood of Halifax. Nova Scotia thus appears to claim an early and special connection with the cause of deaf-mute education in America.

To Nova Scotia, the smallest of the Provinces originally embraced in the Dominion of Canada, we believe belongs the honour of being the foremost among the British Colonies, practically to recognize the claims of the deaf and dumb to a share in the educational privileges, so long exclusively enjoyed by others It is true, that the old Canadian Parlia-

ment, as early as 1854, voted a sum of $80,000 (never expended) for the erection of asylums for the deaf and dumb and the blind, but owing to political changes and complications, nothing was done by the larger and wealthier province commensurate with its resources, or the magnitude and importance of the work. Beyond aiding to a limited extent the Roman Catholic school for deaf-mutes at Montreal, and that founded and conducted by Mr. J. B. McGann, in the upper province, Canada failed to recognize her obligations in reference to the education of her mute population, until 1870 when the present noble instituiton at Belleville was established by the Ontario Legislature, and education made free to all the deaf-mutes of Ontario, a result largely due, we believe, to the enthusiastic and indefatigable efforts of Mr. McGann. Since that time under the energetic principalship of Dr. W. J. Palmer the institution has progressed with almost unexampled rapidity.

The Toronto School—founded by Mr. McGann and subsequently removed to Hamilton—was not opened until some time after we had commenced operations in Halifax. The Halifax School began in August, 1856, that of Toronto, not until 1858.

The history and progress of the Halifax Institution, while presenting many tokens of Divine goodness, afford an encouraging illustration of what may be accomplished, by patient, steady, persevering, and yet quiet and unostentatious effort. Obsure and humble in its origin, this work was not ushered into existence amid the "pomp and circumstance" of public demonstration, the smiles of wealth, the patronage of rank, or the plaudits of enthutiastic multitudes. Small, feeble, and insignificant in its beginning—appealing to none of those sentiments of national honour, or personal interest, which exercise so large an influence in the inception and prosecution of many enterprises, even of a benevolent character—the Halifax Institution for the Deaf and Dumb has gradually emerged into the light of public favor, and attained a position of usefulness and respectability, such as its most sanguine friends could, perhaps, hardly have anticipated. Meeting as it does an important and acknowledged want in the community, it may now be fairly regarded as "an accomplished fact"—one of the permanent institutions of the country.

The Halifax Institution owes it origin incidentally to Mr. William Gray, a deaf-mute, and a pupil of the well-known Mr. Kinniburgh of the Edinburgh Institution. Emigrating from Scotland, presumably with the expectation of making a fortune in the new world, like others of his compatriots, Mr G. was landed, by stress of circumstances, at

DEAF MUTE EDUCATION.

Halifax in the month of August 1855, and, after working for some time at his trade of tailoring, being thrown out of employment, he conceived, or had suggested to him by a brother-mute and fellow-countryman who happened to be, also residing in Halifax, the idea of opening a school for the deaf and dumb, as a means of subsistence.

His advertisement attracted the attention of the Rev. James C. Cochran, D.D.,—the venerable and devoted Secretary of the Institution—who immediately sought him out, and found him in a mean lodging engaged in teaching one or two mutes, the place being destitute of the common comforts and even necessaries of life. Mr. Cochran's interest in the deaf and dumb had been first awakened, many years before by meeting on board an American steamboat, with the celebrated Laurent Clerc, and accordingly he now set himself to enlist the sympathies of other benevolent persons in Halifax on behalf of the neglected deaf-mutes of his native province, an object in which he was providentially successful. Along with Andrew Mackinlay, Esq., Custos of the County—and, for many years afterwards the esteemed Chairman of the Board of Directors—he succeeded in obtaining for the infant cause the notice and support of the Legislature and the community, organized a Board of Management, and took other steps for the proper establishment and equipment of the school.

The first Legislative aid was a grant of 1,200 dollars in the spring of 1857, the grant, in subsequent years, being enlarged to 1,600 dollars and 2,000 dollars, as the value and claims of the object became better understood. This, with the voluntary contributions readily obtained, enabled the promoters of the infant institution to provide more suitable accommodation for the school, and to engage Mr. J. Scott Hutton, then and for ten years previously an instructor in the Edinburgh Intitution, as Principal—Mr. Gray, being retained as assistant teacher.

Bringing from Scotland the needful books and apparatus for the work kindly donated by kindred Institutions in the mother country—to the value of about two hundred dollars—Mr. Hutton entered on his duties in Halifax on the 4th of August 1857, with FOUR pupils. The year following the attendance having increased to TWENTY-SEVEN, additional accommodation was procured, a Matron engaged, and the gernarl management then, for the first time, placed in the hands of the Principal and Matron, who henceforward resided in the same building with the pupils—the school previously, being only a Day School, with three or

DEAF MUTE EDUCATION.

four of the boys boarding in the house of the assistant-teacher—and others with friends in the city.

At the close of the first regular session of the school, as an organized institution, in July, 1858, a public meeting on its behalf was held in the Mechanic's Institute, presided over by Mr. A. Mackinlay, Esq., President of the Board, and attended by the Bishop of Nova Scotia and other prominent citizens, when for the first time before a Halifax audience, an exhibition of the method and results of deaf-mute instruction was given in the examination of the pupils, which brought the condition and claims of the deaf and dumb more impressively before the community, and gave a valuable impulse to the new cause.

During the summer vacation immediately following, the Principal, accompanied by several of the pupils, undertook the first of a series of annual tours in the Provinces of Nova Scotia, New Brunswick and Prince Edward Island, addressing public meetings and holding exhibitions on behalf of the Institution, in the principal towns and villages, with gratifying results in the awakening of interest in a department of benevolent effort new to the great body of the people—the accession of new pupils, and the replenishing of the funds.

The first spontaneous movement in the Province, in aid of the Institution, took place on the historic shores of Cobequid Bay, among the intelligent and thriving population of Noel, in the county of Hants, where a bazaar was held in July of this year, at which the Principal and several of the pupils were present by invitation, an occasion memorable to the writer as the first on which he had the privilege of advocating the claims of the deaf and dumb before a rural audience in the Maritime Provinces. About two hundred and fifty dollars was realised by this effort, under all the circumstances a most creditable and cheering result.

In November of the same year (1858) the proceeds amounting to 1,600 dollars of a bazaar in Halifax, under the patronage of the Countess of Mulgrave, lady of his Excellency the Lieut.-Governor, enabled the Directors to purchase the premises, previously rented—but, in the ensuing year, embracing a favorable opportunity, the property was disposed of by the Board, and in August, 1859, the present premises, formerly known as Brunswick Villa, commanding a magnificent view of the noble harbor and surrounding country, were purchased for six thousand and four hundred dollars—a step which proved highly advantageous to the interests of the institution.

DEAF MUTE EDUCATION.

On the 17th of February, 1859, a second exhibition of the school was held in the Mechanic's Institute to a crowded and deeply interested audience, and by request, repeated on the 14th of March in the Temperance Hall, the largest public hall in the city, which was filled to its capacity by a congregation representing all classes and creeds in the community drawn together by the rapidly growing interest felt in the work.

During the Legislative session, the same spring, we had the honor of giving our first exhibition before the members of both branches of the Legislature, on the floors of the House of Assembly, to which, in connection with similar exhibitions in subsequent sessions, may be justly attributed the promotion of that spirit of hearty liberality uniformly displayed by the Legislature of Nova Scotia towards the institution.

In the spring of 1860, the teaching staff was strengthened by the accession of the Principal's father, Mr. George Hutton, for nearly forty years engaged in the instruction of the deaf and dumb in Scotland. Mr. Hutton removed with his family to Nova Scotia, in response to his son's pressing invitation and appeal for aid, at a time when the funds were inadequate to meet the expense of an additional salaried teacher urgently required, and for ten years, till his death in 1870, gave his voluntary services to the Institution without stated remuneration. In 1862 an act of incorporation was obtained from the Legislature for the greater stability of the institution.

Additions and improvements on the premises have been made from time to time to meet the growing necessities of the work. In 1864-5 a new school-room and dormitory were added to the building, with other improvements, at a cost of over $3,000. And, again in 1874 extensive alterations and additions were made, including hospital accommodations and heating apparatus, at an expense of about $9,000. These changes have about doubled the original extent of the building, besides providing for the increased comfort and efficiency of the establishment.

During the last twenty years deputations from the institution have visited every section of Nova Scotia, and P. E. Island, most of New Brunswick, and part of Newfoundland, bringing the claims of the deaf and dumb before the people and awakening an interest in the cause. In this work nearly 11,000 miles have been travelled, between 300 and 400 public meetings held, and nearly $9,000 collected for the funds of institution. The time occupied in these periodical journeys amounts to about SEVENTY-FOUR WEEKS, or nearly a year and a half.

DEAF MUTE EDUCATION.

By these and similar efforts the Governments of the four Maritime Provinces have been enlisted in the cause of deaf-mute education. Nova Scotia led the way in 1857, the first year of the institution; New Brunswick followed in 1860, Prince Edward Island in 1866, and Newfoundland in 1877, thus completing the circle of "Maritime Union" in this philanthropic enterprise. Within twenty years Nova Scotia has contributed $47,000, New Brunswick a little over $8,000, P. E. Island between $3,000 and 4,000 and Newfoundland $500, for the support of the institution.

Of the two rival systems of deaf-mute instruction—the " French " or mimetic, and the " German " or oral method—the preference is given in the Halifax School to the French system, as in our opinion best adapted to promote the intellectual, moral, and religious welfare of the majority of deaf-mutes, and as having the preponderating weight of professional experience in England and America on its side. Oral instruction is given however to semi-mutes and such toto deaf-mutes as show an aptitude for it. Articulation (oral language and lip-reading) is regarded as an accomplishment for the minority, rather than as a basis of education for all.

The average cost per head of maintenance and education in the Halifax Institution has been considerably lower than in perhaps any similar institution in America. In Ontario the average cost is about $170 per pupil and in the United States the per capita cost ranges from about $160 to $300 a year.

It appears that the number of deaf-mutes received into this institution since its first opening in 1856 has been one hundred and ninety-four, of whom 118 were males and 76 females.

Twenty of former pupils are married, as follows—married to deaf-mute partners, 13; married to hearing partners, 7. From these 20 marriages there have been about 22 children born, four of whom are dead, and of those now alive only one shares the infirmity of the parents, who in this case are both congenital deaf-mutes. Deaf-dumbness does not appear to be necessarily hereditary. Statistics on this point in connection with other institutions give the proportion of deaf-mute children of deaf-mute parents as about eight per cent.

THE END.

www.ingramcontent.com/pod-product-compliance
Lightning Source LLC
Chambersburg PA
CBHW022139160426
43197CB00009B/1357